The
Your Father
Never
Taught You

The Things Your Father Never Taught You

Robert Masello

A Perigee Book

A Perigee Book
Published by The Berkley Publishing Group
200 Madison Avenue
New York, NY 10016

Copyright © 1995 by Robert Masello

Book design by Irving Perkins Associates

Cover design by James R. Harris

Cover illustration by Mario Deaudoin

First edition: December 1995

Published simultaneously in Canada.

Library of Congress Cataloging-in-Publication Data

Masello, Robert.
   The things your father never taught you / Robert Masello.
      p.   cm.
   ISBN 0-399-52168-2 (pbk.)
   1. Men—Life skills guides.   2. Life skills—Handbooks, manuals, etc.   I. Title.
   HQ1090.M38   1995
   646.7′0081—dc20   95-12474

Printed in the United States of America.

10   9   8   7   6   5   4   3   2   1

For my father,
who taught me to carry a comb in my pocket,
money in my shoe,
and a song in my heart.

Contents

Acknowledgments

While much of the information in this book is a matter of informed opinion (mostly mine, I'm afraid), I have consulted a number of authorities in their respective fields.

On questions of law, Susan Williams, a distinguished attorney, currently practicing in Los Angeles.

On tax and accounting practices, Mark Neuman, C.P.A.

On Yiddish, the esteemed linguistics scholar Jeffrey Melvoin.

On Chinese table etiquette, Madame Wu, proprietress of Madame Wu's Garden, in Santa Monica.

On American music, Chuck Cohen.

On Eastern philosophy, William Bleich.

As is customary, I'd like to say that these respected sources are in no way responsible for any mistakes which may appear in the text. (I didn't pay them anything, I can hardly blame them if there's a problem.) The buck stops with me.

But with this one disclaimer: rather than acting solely on the counsel contained in this book, please confer with your own physician, lawyer, tax planner, dentist, personal trainer, psychic, etc., before taking any serious course of action. Your case might not have been covered, or referred to, here. This book provides only general advice and guidelines.

Enough said. (If I'm not covered now, I never will be.)

Introduction

He taught you to throw a baseball.

And part your hair.

To drive a car.

And help a lady on with her coat.

But where was Dad when you had to throw your very first dinner party? Or mix your first martini?

And why didn't he tell you about stuff like office politics, and room service?

Where was he when your tax return got audited?

Or your luggage got lost?

And how come he never said a word—not one word—about how to hold a pair of chopsticks in the classical Chinese fashion?

Dad's a great guy—there's no denying it—but there are still certain things he probably overlooked. Certain skills a modern man absolutely must possess. Answers a sophisticated guy must know. Manners he must display.

Here, such things are neatly assembled. Here, you'll find all the things that Dad didn't know (like how to beat jet lag), never understood (if fluoride is really necessary), or just plain didn't want to talk about (whether or not you should have an affair with somebody you work with).

Here, you'll find an indispensable guide to staying in

style, staying in shape, and staying on top, from the board-room to the bedroom.

And maybe you'll even discover something you can turn around and share with Dad. He's never too old to learn, you know.

The Things
Your Father
Never
Taught You

CHAPTER I

At Home

"A King may make a nobleman, but he cannot make a gentleman."

—EDMUND BURKE

Living It Up

If a man's home is his castle, ask yourself this: why are you living in a dungeon?

You're still young, you have the world before you, things are only going to keep right on getting better. You'll be getting promotions, pay hikes, bigger challenges, greater opportunities. Why, just because you're not earning a lot right now, should you fritter away these years living in anything less than you can afford?

To my mind, there's no reason at all.

Living right up to—but not beyond—your means serves several useful purposes. For one, a man is known by the address he keeps. In both social and business settings, it pays to be able to say you live in the right part of town—women will be impressed, business contacts will think you must be some kind of wunderkind, family and friends will want to kick themselves for being so wrong about you. Based on nothing more than a number and the name of a street, everyone will form a more favorable impression of you.

And that includes you. If you live in a crummy part of town, chances are your apartment will be crummy, your neighbors will be crummy, and you'll feel crummy about living there. All in all, this is a recipe for low self-esteem and impending failure. Should a future chairman of the board have to bang on the radiator pipes to get heat, or light a match every time he wants to turn on the stove? Face it—if you're not prepared to invest in your future, who else will be?

This holds true for both renters and buyers. If you're renting, you're just passing through—so why not pass the time pleasantly, with all the amenities, a view perhaps, and a doorman who tips his cap? The time you spend here will never be more than an interlude in your life; make it one you can enjoy looking back on.

If you're buying, either an apartment or a house, re-member the first three rules of real estate: location, location, location. You're better off with the worst piece of property in a great area than you are with the best piece of property in a lousy area—if you don't believe this, just wait till you try to sell.

Or until you find your car radio missing . . . for the third time.

And finally, understand that when a real estate broker tells you that a neighborhood is "gentrifying," it doesn't mean that the place is going to be showing up in next month's issue of *Town and Country*. More likely, it means that the gang warfare has simmered down lately, maybe even enough for trained police observers to predict, with some confidence, which gang will be the winner. Either way, the winner won't be you.

Energy Savers

Depending on the strength of your mystical bent (do you read your horoscope for fun, or for serious career advice?), you may or may not elect to incorporate the mysterious principles of feng shui into your home design.

But just in case . . .

Literally, feng shui means "wind and water," and it might be described as the ancient Chinese science of energy conservation; according to the Taoist wise men, there is life energy, or "chi," all around us. If you want to retain this energy, and use it to improve your own life and good fortune, you must lay out and furnish your home in such a way as to capture as much of this vital chi as you can. If you don't, it will literally fly out the door.

So, the first thing to do is to check the front door. Is there a street running straight toward it? This is very bad news, lots of negative chi. To deflect this bad energy, hang a small mirror on the outside of the door.

Next, place a wind chime near the door, and ring it at least a couple of times each day. This will lift your spirits, and any others lurking in the house.

If you have any windows facing north, shut them. This will help to preserve the positive chi in your house. So will putting a green plant in the other windows.

If you've got any dead plants around, or even dried flowers that have lost their luster, toss them. They're an energy drain.

So are toilets. If you want to keep your money or good fortune from surging down the tubes every time you flush, hang a lush green plant in the bathroom, ideally above the tank itself. Even paintings of flowers in bloom can help.

In the bedroom be sure to place the bed in what's known as the "command position," catercorner to the door; you'll sleep better and wake up feeling more refreshed. If you do this, and you still don't wake up feeling bright-eyed and bushy-tailed, then there may be something more seriously amiss with your chi; a specialist should be called.

The Green Indoors

Wondering if you should bother with houseplants? Perhaps the best reason to keep them around is not for what they add to the decor, but for what they say about you as a person: any man who cares enough to keep a living thing alive—a living thing, furthermore, that doesn't catch Frisbees or mice—is automatically considered gentle, nurturing, and deeply in touch with his feminine side.

So if you're an insensitive lout, buy a plant, stick it on the coffee table, and let it work its magic on your female guests.

Your only problem will be keeping the damned thing green. Some pointers that might help:

Care and Cultivation

Two things are essential to plant life: one is water, the other is light. (Don't you wish everything could be that simple?)

The light should be neither too bright nor too dim. Indirect, natural lighting is what you want.

If the plant is getting too much light, it will probably wilt and its color will start to disappear. If it's getting too little, its leaves will elongate, or give up and fall off altogether.

As for water: give it too little and the thing croaks; too much and it drowns. Using tepid water, give your plant a good dousing; pour enough water into the soil that it trickles all the way down to the roots. Then, after the pot has drained, toss out the water the plant is sitting in.

Later on, to see how the moisture is holding up, stick your finger into the soil and see how it feels. A swamp? Or the Sahara? If the leaves of the plant have turned yellow and hang down like a basset hound's ears, you're probably overdoing the water. If the leaves are turning brown and collecting on the carpet, you're not providing enough. Rule of thumb: many plants go into a kind of winter hibernation, so give them less water then.

If you're feeling particularly attentive, you can (a) spritz your plant several times a day with a mister, (b) sponge off the leaves now and then, to remove dust and dirt, and (c) tell it what happened to you at work that day. (The scientific community is still divided on the utility of talking to plants, but in the meantime, how can it hurt?)

Going away on a business trip? (Perhaps you shouldn't mention this to the plant.) Wrap the whole plant, loosely, in a plastic bag, into which you've poked several holes. Then water the plant very thoroughly. Leave it where it will receive sufficient light. And, assuming you know its tastes, tune the radio to the appropriate station and leave it on low.

Low-Maintenance Plant Life

Asparagus fern. Give it ordinary dirt, and some indirect sun, and it'll hang out in a hanging pot indefinitely. Between waterings, let the soil dry out.

Staghorn fern. This one doesn't even need soil. You can hang it on a wall, in medium filtered sunlight, and give it frequent mistings with water and plant food solution.

Bromeliad. Likes moisture, warm temps. There's a little cup-like spot near the center—that's where to pour the water.

Ficus. Given medium to good light, and a steady level of moisture at the roots, this'll grow tall. Handles air conditioning with aplomb.

Palm. Also fine with AC. Keep the plant in shade and evenly damp.

Chinese evergreen. Survives most anything, including meager light. Between soakings, let the soil dry out.

Rubber plant. Keep it out of direct sunlight, rinse the leaves off now and then, and pinch it back if it starts to get so tall it's tilting.

Grape ivy. A member of the Cissus family, this one is much easier to grow than English ivy. Medium light, frequent mistings. Let soil dry out between waterings.

African violets. Never let 'em dry out, never let 'em get too cold or hot, and they'll never let you down. They bloom nearly all year.

Geranium. This one revels in sunshine and medium water. To produce flowers, it's got to be potted.

Philodendron. Given its druthers, it likes warm weather and pretty good light. But it'll make do with almost any conditions at all.

Spider plants. Also good under almost any conditions—but they prefer a sunny, airy spot.

Peace lily. Lovely and green if kept in indirect light. But capable of producing beautiful lily-like blooms if given gobs of light, along with moist soil and weekly infusions of plant food.

The Compleat Kitchen

If you're a summa cum laude graduate of the Cordon Bleu, skip this section altogether. I have nothing to say to you.

But if you subsist on take-out and Granola bars, if your idea of a home-cooked meal says Swanson anywhere on it, if the words "colander" and "coriander" mean the same thing to you (nothing), then perhaps you will gain something from what follows.

One reason the kitchen may be such a user-unfriendly area for you is that you haven't taken the time to outfit it properly. Sure, preparing food is no fun, but cutting vegetables with a penknife or straining spaghetti with a squash racket (and here's where that colander could come in handy) only makes it needlessly hard. A small complement of kitchen items—purchased for a relatively small investment—can make your visits to the kitchen more pleasant, more productive, and as a result, more frequent.

You might even learn to cook a few things.

The Fundamentals

· A wooden cutting board, of a generous size. But wash it with warm, soapy water every now and then—and *always* after you've cut raw meat on it.

· A decent set of knives. There are different knives, believe it or not, for chopping, slicing, carving, paring, etc.

Good ones, from companies like Henckels and Wusthof, come in sets all made up for you, and once you've got them you should make them easily accessible by leaving them on the counter in a wooden rack or by hanging them on one of those magnetic wall holders.

But don't put them in the dishwasher. Wash them by hand and dry them immediately.

• A timer. There's probably one built into your oven, but you may never learn how to use it. Or you'll try, and it will ding forever. Buy one of those little white wind-up models.

• A spatula. While metal's more official, the Teflon-coated kind won't scratch any of your pots and pans.

• A set of long-handled instruments. Namely, a fork, a spoon, and a perforated spoon. Keep these handy, too. (If any of these is made of wood, keep it out of the dishwasher, which can dry it up and crack it.)

• A colander. Yes, this is the metal strainer you use for spaghetti, etc. But don't get the kind with one long handle; get the kind with little feet, so it can stand on its own. You want both your hands free to pour the boiling water and pasta into it.

• A cookie sheet. All kinds of things—from pot pies to actual cookies—can sit in the oven on this. And since it will catch drips and spill-overs, it will save you cleaning the oven.

• Liquid and dry measuring cups; a set of measuring spoons. You never know—you may use one of these some-day. A couple of mixing bowls would be good, too.

• Pots and pans. I got all of mine as premiums from opening bank accounts. But banks have pretty much gotten out of that game.

If you're going to buy these items, get at least one skillet with a lid that fits, a pot also with its own lid, and a rectangular roasting pan.

• Casserole dishes. In one- and two-quart sizes, with fitted lids. Get ones that are attractive enough to go straight from oven to table.

• Tupperware. No jokes, please. The resealable plastic container is one of this century's greatest contributions to domestic life (ranking right up there with the VCR and alcohol-free beer). If you are going to cook—even something as simple as tuna noodle casserole—never make enough for just one meal. Or even two. Make a ton. Eat all you can, put some more in the Tupperware, and freeze the rest. (But do remember to label the frozen leftovers, or you will find them months later and have no idea what they ever were.)

Freon Is Your Friend

In all your life, you will never find a buddy as strong and silent, as reliable and at the same time as nonjudgmental, as your refrigerator. Treat it right—which takes almost no thought—and it will always be there for you.

Treat it wrong—and you'll be drinking warm beer.

Let's assume you have a fairly standard model—white, with a freezer compartment upstairs and a larger compartment below. Let's also assume, at the beginning of this exercise, that the fridge is empty and clean. (For the record, a refrigerator works better when there are things inside it—even if it's only your sporting equipment.)

If it's not clean, simply wipe out the racks and bins with a weak solution of baking soda and warm water.

What do you put inside it? If you're seriously entertaining questions of health and longevity, you may use the lower bins for fresh fruits and vegetables.

Very laudable.

If not, you'll find that these bins are, instead, a perfect repository for the take-out menus you usually lose. Keep the take-out menus in the fridge, and the simple logic of hunger will send you back there every time you go looking for them.

The door of the fridge, you'll notice, has plastic compartments: one is marked Dairy. Do you know anyone who keeps a stick of butter in a dish and puts it in there anymore? This compartment is ideal, however, for leftover soy sauce packets, Twix and Snickers bars, and, you may be glad to know, those expensive little camera batteries—did you know that they last longer if kept cold?

What else should you keep in your fridge? At the very least, you always want to keep on hand the basic ingredients for casual, impromptu entertaining:

- soft drinks
- beer
- tonic water, club soda
- a bottle of white wine
- olives
- a slab of cheese (not the kind that comes in single-slice servings). Brie is boring but fine; a jarlsberg is a little more interesting; chèvre has a touch of class. Do check the cheese every few weeks, however; if it's fuzzier than your tennis balls, it's time to get a replacement.

The freezer is, for many men, a glacial waste, fit only for ice cubes and a bottle of vodka whose top becomes so frozen it can't be unscrewed. But in this, the Age of the Microwave, there's no excuse for that attitude. A small supply of Hungry Man dinners can come in awfully handy on a night when you're too tired to lift the phone; two or three of them might almost make a meal. Also, be advised that nuts stored in the freezer will keep longer, and they'll be easier to crack. Coffee—ground or instant—will keep fresh in here, and candles (if you're planning a slow seduction) will burn less quickly if they've been frozen stiff first.

Maintenance

Although the refrigerator is as commonly ignored as a college loan, it's best to offer it a little routine care.

If you smell an odor, check first to see if there's any food well past its prime. Then try swabbing out the bins and inside walls. If this doesn't work either, check the drip pan underneath; it may have caught some food spills that need to be rinsed out.

Be sure to wipe any dirt or grime off the gasket (or door seal); if the gasket's not firm, cold air could be escaping. To test the seal, try closing the fridge door on a paper towel; if you can easily pull out the towel, the gasket's not doing its job, and you need to clean it, and tighten the door hinges.

And though I know you won't want to hear this, it's also a good idea to clean the condenser coils (which disperse the heat) once or twice a year. Located either under the fridge (where they're difficult to reach) or in the back (where they're quite impossible), they tend to collect dust, which reduces their efficiency and raises the cost of running the fridge. Get a condenser-coil cleaning brush (most hardware stores carry them), and with the help, too, of the crevice tool on your vacuum cleaner, clean off the coils. A good time to do this is just before the hot summer months hit.

If your refrigerator is a frost-free model, you're in clover. If it's not, you'll have to defrost the freezer now and again. Plan to do this a few days ahead of time, so you can eat and drink everything that's perishable. Then turn the dial to defrost, and let the dripping begin. Do not become impatient and start hacking at the ice with a carving knife. You can inadvertently do some serious damage. Nor should you try leaving the blow-dryer in there to heat things up. For some reason, blow-dryers expire this way. (Trust me, I've lost two.) The ice will melt in its own good time.

The Bathroom

It's not as if you sleep in here. Or entertain. Or watch TV. So when it comes to bathroom maintenance, why should you have to do anything more than occasionally swab the petrified shaving cream off the counter and change the towel?

Why? Because your bathroom is the one place you will definitely have to visit at least once or twice a day. You may eat all your meals out, you may sleep on the sofa, but there's no way to skip the bathroom break.

Nor will your guests be able to skip it. If you're even *thinking* about getting that certain someone into the bedroom, you'd better be darn sure first that the bathroom is not enough to make her shudder. If she can't pry that sliver of Zest off the soap dish without breaking a nail, she won't ever want to see the state that your sheets are in.

(Sheets—we'll get to that later.)

In the bathroom, you must—and there can be no dissension on this score—provide a clean, fresh, dry, guest towel, clearly displayed for that purpose, on a towel bar near the sink.

You must provide a bar of soap new enough that it bears some faint resemblance to the shape it came in. Or else a liquid soap dispenser, the sides of which are not coated with uncaught drips.

You must provide a mirror sufficiently clean that a woman could check her makeup in it without wearing a miner's cap.

You must provide, to borrow a phrase, a clean, well-lighted place. Any woman even contemplating spending the night will be factoring in a shower the next morning, and if she's afraid the moss growing on the roof of your shower stall is going to land in her hair, you can bet she'll elect to sleep in her own little bed that night.

Besides clean towels and a bathmat, what else do you need? A well-supplied medicine chest. What should such a chest contain?

For unexpected guests, a spare toothbrush (and that means still in the wrapper, not the brush you once used for grouting).

A tube of toothpaste that you haven't yet begun to curl from the bottom.

For your own everyday use, a complete medicine cabinet should hold, in addition to the usual shaving paraphernalia and ordinary items such as aspirin and deodorant, the following:

- rubbing alcohol for muscle aches and bruises
- iodine for cuts
- petroleum jelly for burns and abrasions
- Band-Aids in assorted sizes

- prescription and nonprescription medicines that haven't expired (after their expiration dates, some medications decay, and some actually get stronger, so discard them either way)
- stomach settlers, something like Pepto-Bismol or Alka-Seltzer
- Tylenol, or some other nonaspirin painkiller
- tweezers, nail clippers, Q-tips, an emery board, small scissors
- a natural-bristle hairbrush (for more on this, see "Brushing Up")

In the Arms of Morpheus

Like it or not, most of what goes on in the bedroom is deadly dull—you're lying there, eyes closed, breathing deeply, dreaming of things that will never be and women you'll never meet. (I mean, what are the chances—honestly—that you'll be the pilot on a flight to the moon and that your sole passenger, Cindy Crawford, will implore you to teach her the wonders of weightless sex?)

Given the true nature of what transpires here, it's a wonder so many men go to all the trouble and expense of furnishing their bedrooms with black satin sheets, leather headboards, and mirrored ceilings. These accoutrements will excite no one. Tactless women will laugh out loud; tactful ones will laugh on the phone, later, when they call their friends.

Never give anyone reason to make such a call.

Your bedroom should not be treated as the Lair of Love; if you can even imagine Bob Guccione curling up in here with a good book, you're doing it wrong.

Nor should it look like a flophouse, with a twisted gray

sheet trailing off the foam mattress and an empty soup can with a spoon in it sitting on the floor. (What would your mother say?)

Regardless of what you wish would happen in here, or who you hope to one day entice inside, your bedroom is, first and foremost, the place you go for rest and rejuvenation. It should be, above all, comfortable, consoling, peaceful. This is the inner sanctum, where the body is restored and the spirit takes refuge. The *Friday the 13th* poster should definitely go.

So what should—and what shouldn't—your bedroom contain? Let's begin with the basics:

A nightstand. And by this, I don't mean the cardboard box your stereo speakers came in. A real table, of wood or metal (it's up to you), but one which has at least one shelf and one drawer. On top of it you should keep the essentials—a box of Kleenex, an alarm clock, a decent lamp if you like to read in bed, the remote control if you've got a TV in here. The drawer is for more personal items: your diary, if you keep one, and condoms (you never know).

A bed. Unless you're studying to become a Trappist monk, you'll want to get something more than a single bed. A double, or queen-size, you'll find, is neither too big for one person, nor too small for two. But whatever the size, don't skimp on the mattress and box spring (also known as a "sleep set," in industry parlance). Get them firm, and get them durable. If you don't get a good night's sleep, everything else in your life will suffer—including those who have to deal with you the next day.

A dresser. Some men think this a frivolous piece of furniture. Why bother when the room already has a closet and the

Exercycle has handlebars perfect for hanging? Get a dresser, with at least three generous drawers. Anything that doesn't normally go on a hanger goes in here—and that includes T-shirts, underpants, folded shirts, socks, handkerchiefs, swimming trunks, etc. And possibly . . .

Pajamas. Yes, pjs. The modern man should own at least two pairs—one in lightweight cotton, one in something warmer, like flannel. Why? Because even if you never wear them when alone, you should have them in case you are (a) invited to a friend's country house, (b) unexpectedly admitted to the hospital, or (c) entertaining a new female friend in front of whom you are not yet comfortable wearing the hockey jersey you usually sleep in. The pjs are also something you can offer to her if she is debating whether or not to spend the night at all: this at least solves the sleepwear question.

Addendum: Making the Bed

This is one of those repetitive chores that seem, in the long run, to be so futile. Why make the bed each morning when you're only going to mess it up again that night? And, admittedly, there is an irresistible logic to that.

But resist it.

A home with an unmade bed looks slovenly; a home with a made bed signals order, maturity, organization. A man with a made bed is, by extension, a man who changes his underwear, calls his aged mother, is kind to dogs and children. For the minute it takes each day, it's worth all the good advertising it provides.

A minute? Yes. One reason you may resist making the bed is unhappy memories of having to do it right—making hospital corners at summer camp, or getting the top blanket taut enough to bounce a quarter on, or fixing the sheet so it neatly folds back beneath the pillows. You're making this job harder than it has to be. To render it as effortless as possible:

• Buy fitted sheets. If you have trouble wrestling them onto the mattress, do alternate corners—top right, then bottom left, bottom right, then top left. If you buy linen or cotton, they'll feel great—cooler in summertime—but they'll require ironing. (Shudder.) A pure polyester will require no ironing, but you will have to wring out the sweat each morning. For relative comfort and ease of care, you may always opt for a cotton/poly combo.

• Consider skipping traditional blankets and bed-spreads. Simply purchase a big white down comforter, which, with one quick unfurling each day, will fall across your bed and lie there happily, with no corners to be tucked in and no borders to be turned down.

• Make sure your comforter has an easily removed, and washable, cover; if it doesn't, get one for it. True, it's a nuisance, removing the cover every few weeks, laundering it, and then zipping or buttoning it back on again, but you really shouldn't be sleeping with cracker crumbs, wine stains, and sloughed-off skin cells. It's unhygienic.

• Buy good pillows. A recent medical study done at Johns Hopkins suggested that "nocturnal neck posture" contributed to the chronic headaches and neck pain suffered by a lot of people: "Moreover, the neck discomfort can cause inability to fall asleep, sleep fragmentation, subsequent diurnal tiredness and drowsiness." Enough said? There's a lot of news on the pillow front these days, with manufacturers promoting everything from cervical roll pillows, which fit neatly under your head and neck, to "water pillows." (Remember water beds? Maybe it's best we forget.) Find a pillow that's right for you—Does it give you the support you need? Are you allergically unaffected by its contents? Is it big enough?—and use it. Research has shown that stomach-sleepers prefer soft pillows, back-sleepers prefer mediums, and side-sleepers prefer firm.

Whatever your own preference, some allergists recommend that, due to the potential problems caused by the buildup of bacteria-laden dust, you replace the pillow with a new one every three to five years. By then it's probably lost its oomph anyway.

Sweet Dreams

There are two kinds of people in this world—the kind who put their heads on the pillow and fall instantly asleep, and the kind who put their heads on the pillow, twist, turn, flop around, get up, eat a blintz, get back in bed, replay that argument with the boss, turn on the TV, watch the last half of a *Twilight Zone*, turn off the TV, stare at the ceiling, turn on the light, read the sports section of yesterday's newspaper, turn off the light, sock the pillow, count sheep, and eventually, about three hours before the alarm is set to go off . . . go to sleep.

Which kind are you?

If you're the first kind, you are blessed.

If you're the second kind, here's what you have to do to start getting the rest you need.

· Get some physical exercise during the day. It de-stresses you. But don't do your exercising within three hours of bedtime—if it's that close, it can leave you all pumped up, not deflated.

• Stop smoking, drink no caffeine for six hours before bed, and don't drink any alcohol within three hours. (Yes, alcohol can knock you out, but if that's how you put yourself to sleep, there's a very good chance you'll wake up a few hours later, totally discombobulated.)

• Invent some relaxing routine that you can follow, every night, to prepare for bed. A warm bath is good, a meditation break, listening to some music (not Metallica). Whatever it is, try to stick to it. It'll soon become a kind of signal to your body to slow down and chill out.

• Stop confusing your bedroom with your office, dining room, or den. Don't use it to (a) watch videotapes, which can absorb you past your bedtime, (b) read novels, which can keep you up turning the pages, (c) do paperwork, which can drag you right back into the minutiae of the day. Do those things elsewhere. Make the bedroom the place you go for only two things: romantic endeavors (which can have their own soporific effects) and sleep.

• Make the room quiet, and make it dark. If there's ambient noise that can disturb or distract you, run the air conditioner or get a white noise machine. If streetlight filters in through the blinds, get curtains. If the curtains are sheer, get thicker ones.

• As a last resort, and only after consulting your doctor, you can try some medications to help you sleep. (But once the medications get you on track, and on a regular sleep schedule, cut them out.) Most of the over-the-counter drugs, such as Benadryl, contain antihistamines, which can make you drowsy. There's also a raft of prescription sleep aids, including Xanax, Valium, Halcion, and a newcomer named Ambien; synthetic melatonin, being promoted as the "natural" sleep aid, is also in the works. But they can all prove addictive, and they can all have side effects, from memory impairment to sluggishness. So use them with caution, and only after the simpler solutions have failed.

• Establish and maintain a regular sleep schedule, getting up and going to bed at the same times every day. Your body clock needs to get set—and it needs to be kept that way.

The Sounds of Silence

One man's music, as they say, is another man's noise.

So how do you keep your neighbor's racket out of your ears?

The first remedy is the civil one: a polite knock on the door, a polite request that he turn down the stereo, and a polite return to your own domicile.

If that doesn't work, there's always a polite call to the police (who will, unfortunately, show up hours later, and regard you as more of a nuisance than your neighbor).

Then there's the letter of complaint you can file with the appropriate city or county agencies.

But the wheels of justice grind exceedingly slow, and if you need more immediate relief, you may wish to consider:

• Heavy drapes, thick carpets, upholstered furniture. All of these muffle and absorb ambient sound.

• Weather stripping and sealers around your windows, doors, and walls. To keep as much of the sound outside as possible. Windows can also be double-paned.

- Camouflage. A whirring fan, humming air conditioner, or low-volume music of your own (that New Age stuff seems to have been invented for this purpose) can provide "white noise" that masks the annoying outside sounds.

- Earplugs. If they fit well, they can cut noise levels by about 30 decibels. (But you do have to listen to the boom-boom-booming of your own heart.)

- Headphones. Tune in to your own music (but miss all your phone calls).

- Payback. Your neighbor still blasting the sweet sounds of the Atomic Terminators? Place your own speakers against his wall, or face down on your floor (if he lives below). Then insert, in your automatic tape-reverse deck, Dvořák's *Serenade for Strings*. Turn the volume to the max, close your door, and take a week's vacation by the sea.

The Home Office

Sometimes your home is your office. You're either "between assignments," as they say, or you've decided to join the burgeoning entrepreneurial ranks. No more being just a part of the flock—now you're going to fly solo, a lone eagle of the sky.

But before you do, you must get your work nest in order.

What You Need

First, you've got to set aside a space for your work—a space that serves no other purpose. If you've got a spare room, great. If not, partition off a part of some room—even if you have to do it with shoji screens. There are a couple of reasons for this: for one, you need the psychological reinforcement of having one place where your business is done—and where, when you leave it, your work is left behind. Otherwise, working at home can become working all the time.

For another, if you're working from home, you'll want to take a deduction on your taxes based on the amount of your living area reserved exclusively for business. In many cases, you can also deduct the appropriate portion of your other household expenses, such as electricity. But before they allow this, the IRS likes to see walls and doors around your work area; they don't like to see TVs in there, or beds, or refrigerators, or exercise bikes. All work and no play—that's their motto, and you'd better live up to it.

Get whatever you need in the way of office equipment and supplies, and don't stint on the expense here. (These are cut-and-dried deductions.) If you're going to go for it and start up the next Microsoft, then go for it—don't hamstring your own efforts by typing on an old Corona and filing your papers in shopping bags. Time is money, too—surely you've heard that—and you don't want to spend your time rummaging around for a paper you need, or dabbing Wite-Out over your typos.

Get a fax machine—it is now considered a required component of virtually any business—and don't believe it when the salesman tells you that you can install it on your regular phone line because it has an automatic switching capacity. It doesn't. The only way to keep a fax working properly is to put it on a dedicated line. At first, you'll resist, thinking, "How many faxes do I get anyway?" Then, after the thirty-fourth time you're interrupted on a phone call by a persistent beeping from a fax someone is trying to send you, you'll break down and order another line. Do it at the beginning, and you won't have to call all your clients later to apprise them of the new fax number.

What You Need to Do

Alert all your potential clients or customers to your new business—and warn off your friends.

The moment you announce you are working from home, many of your friends will assume you are now a man of leisure, someone they can call up in the middle of the day to shoot the breeze with. Your family will assume you are available to run errands. Your neighbors will figure they can leave word with the UPS delivery man that you'll be home to sign for their packages. The girl across the hall will want to know if you can feed her cat while she's away for a few days.

You are not retired—you are at work.

While the world does all it can to deny it, you must preserve a strong sense of yourself as a businessperson. Just because you're not driving to an office every morning doesn't mean you should slouch around in an old bathrobe all day. Sure, you can skip the suit and tie, but get up, shave, get dressed. Behave, in all outward respects, as an upright, functioning member of human society; if you start to slide, you'll find yourself letting your fingernails curl and your hair grow shaggy before you know it. Soon you'll be taping foil over the windows to ward off the alien mind-control waves.

Get out at least once a day. Meet a client for lunch. Make an appointment to drum up some new business.

Stick to a schedule. Go into your home office every day at 9:30 (or whenever) and stay in there during what would be usual business hours. You not only need to do it to make sure the work gets done—you need to keep your own schedule roughly attuned to the rest of the workaday world. Under normal circumstances, you can't field business calls at midnight, or win a new contract at 6 A.M.

And finally, you want to have a set time at which you can seriously knock off for the day. Working for yourself can be not only the most rewarding, but the hardest, thing you've ever done—the boss is always there, and he always knows what you're up to. Cut yourself a break. What's the point of working for yourself if you're the worst boss you ever had?

A Place for Everything

How organized are you?

It's a difficult thing to quantify. There are no accepted measures. But can you, without sifting through piles of paper or roaming from room to room, lay your hands on your checkbook, your car keys, your sunglasses? Is the *TV Guide* where you thought it was, are there old magazines cluttering up the coffee table, do you open the door to the hall closet only at your own peril?

If, after consideration of these questions, you concede that your place could benefit from a little more organization than it presently displays, consider these small measures as a step in the right direction:

   • Allot a certain amount of time—even as little as ten minutes—to cleaning up. Much of the time we don't get organized because we're looking at the whole project, at everything that has to be done, and since we know there isn't enough time to do it all, we don't do any of it. You'd be surprised at what you can accomplish in even ten minutes.

   • Instead of trying to do a random, but comprehensive, clean-up, designate a specific area—the kitchen counter, say, or the top of your desk—and devote all your attention to organizing that one spot. This way you won't get sidetracked wandering all over the house, and you'll have something definite to show for yourself when you're done. A neat and clean desk may inspire you to tackle the garage.

• Separate the wheat from the chaff. What do you really need, and what's just taking up space at this point? A rule of thumb for clothes is, if you haven't worn it in a year, toss it. You can make that two years, if you like, but the chances are good that you'll never again put it on. It won't fit, it'll be out of style, or you never really liked it in the first place.

• Handle each piece of paper only once. Although this rule isn't always practicable, the logic behind it is good: if you stay on top of things, they won't mount up. So, when your bank statement arrives, reconcile it with your checkbook that day, then file the statement away. When you get a letter from a friend, answer it—then discard it. If you haven't read a section of the paper, and the next day's edition has already landed on the doorstep, get rid of yesterday's news.

• Keep plenty of good-sized folders and several boxes— those brown banker's boxes, in particular—on hand. Label and date the folders and put into them all the papers you still can't decide what to do with. Then put the folder into one of the banker's boxes. When the box is full, stick it in the basement or the attic. Five years from now, when you next come across it, you'll find it's much easier to throw away the stuff inside.

• Make sure your closet has a good light in it— darkness can conceal a multitude of sins—and plenty of hangers. Many a shirt winds up on a doorknob for want of an extra hanger. When you hang something up, take a second to put it where you'll be easily able to find it again—pants at one end, jackets at the other, shirts and ties in the middle. Instead of kicking off your shoes under the sofa or bed, kick them, if you must, into the bottom of the closet. If you're feeling especially orderly, you might consider a shoe rack.

Clean Sweep

Of all the inane sayings that somehow manage to stay in use, one of the most absurd is "Cleanliness is next to godliness." What, I ask you, is that supposed to mean? That God cares if you clean behind your ears? That He hates a dusty end table? Is that why the world is in such a deplorable state, because God is so busy checking to see if the glasses have water spots that he can't be bothered to worry about little things like pestilence and famine?

If you know the answer to this one, call me.

In the meantime, I'll concede that, godly or not, household cleaning has to be done. Society expects no less of you. So here's what you need to know.

The Cleanup Arsenal

One reason you hate doing household clean-up is that you haven't bothered to go out and get the necessary supplies; with the right stuff on hand, the whole process goes faster and more smoothly. For starters, get hold of:

• Several rolls of two-ply paper towels. The cheap one-ply towels soak up nothing, and make more of a mess than they're worth.

• Loads of clean, dry rags. They're not only softer and more durable than the paper towels, they're also cheaper in the long run. So don't throw out that ragged old cotton shirt; rip off the buttons and recycle it as a rag.

• Some all-purpose cleaner, such as Fantastik, that comes in an easy spray bottle. If you're environmentally aware, I suppose you can buy the refillable spray bottle. (Though it does strike me as odd that after you've refilled the spray bottle, you keep it, but throw away the bottle that the refill came in. Are we accomplishing anything here?)

• An abrasive cleanser, such as Ajax or Comet. They're indispensable in the kitchen and bathroom, but before scrubbing any surface you have your doubts about, read the label on the canister, and if you're still unsure, just rub a little of the cleanser on an inconspicuous area and see what happens.

• Assorted sponges and rugged scrubbing pads. Personally, I use those little yellow Dobie pads, and find they hold up quite well.

• An old toothbrush, for scrubbing away at mildew in the grooves between your bathroom tiles.

• A toilet brush. And I do mean brush, not one of those plastic imitations. You want hard, thick bristles to do the job properly.

• A window cleaner (Windex, or a generic, is fine); a spray disinfectant (Lysol or one of its many brethren); a furniture polish (ever hear of Lemon Pledge?).

• Heavy equipment—a mop, broom, dustpan, pail, and vacuum cleaner. (On the subject of vacuums, let me just add that the hand-held variety—Dust Busters and such—do not qualify. Equipped with the power of one anemic hamster, and the storage capacity of a thimble, they choke and shiver at the first sign of a dangerous dust bunny.)

What to Do

Would it make any impression at all if I said that household cleaning is best done on a regular basis? That it's not a good idea to wait for special occasions, like the repatriation of Hong Kong, the launch of the Mars probe, or the arrival of the new millennium?

If you stay on top of things, you'll find that the cleaning is less arduous. When dust and dirt and grease have time to settle in, to firmly adhere to furniture and countertops and floors, to join with each other and with residual body oil to create new and perplexing recombinant forms, it's just that much harder to scrub and scrape them off.

That said (and I'm sure I've made a powerful impression here), some tips that may streamline the whole cleaning process are:

· If space permits, leave bathroom cleaning supplies in the bathroom, kitchen in the kitchen, etc. Otherwise, keep everything together in one clean, dry, well-ventilated place. Don't let brooms and brushes wear out by resting them on their bristles; hang 'em up.

· When cleaning windows, you can use the specialty pump spray products, a homemade solution of water and vinegar, or a combo of lemon juice and water (four tablespoons of lemon juice to one gallon of water). If the window's not too far gone, just try some tap water. To avoid streaking, don't wash windows in direct sunlight.

When drying the glass, you can resort to the obvious

choices (paper towels or rags), or you can use an old standby—crumpled-up newspaper pages. On the plus side, the newspapers don't leave streaks on the glass; on the debit side, they make a huge wet pile at your feet, and the ink can rub off on your hands and on the wooden window frame.

· TV sets and computer screens serve, by virtue of their static electricity, as magnets for dust and grime. To clean them, turn them off, then wet a soft rag or paper towel with a small amount of glass cleaner. Don't ever spray the stuff on the machine itself. Wipe the surfaces gently.

· Most wooden furniture is well protected by the finish that was originally applied. If you spill something on it, mop up the spill before it has a chance to erode the lacquer. Dust the wood with a soft cloth.

Waxy build-up can indeed pose a problem; if you use furniture polish too often, it can leave a surface residue. So be sparing. If you've got a nick or scratch, you can try to conceal it with a colored polish. Whatever you do, never wipe against the grain.

· When mopping up the inside of a microwave oven, just use tap water, or tap water with a dash of dishwashing liquid added. Keep the sponge damp, not wet, and make sure you get all the crumbs and spatters out; otherwise, they can create an odor problem. Spend an extra few seconds on the door and door seal; if they're not clean and tight, they can allow microwave leakage.

· For mildew, the best offense is a good defense. If you've got a closet where it shows up, for instance, you can raise the temperature inside, and lower the humidity, simply by leaving on a 60-watt bulb at all times. (Just make sure the bulb isn't too close to anything you're storing in there.) The electricity cost will be a few bucks per month.

Otherwise, the best agent to use against mildew is chlorine bleach. But after you've used it (either diluted according to the label directions, or in some specialty bathroom cleaner), be sure to rinse off the mildewed surface. Oh, and just in case you've forgotten your chemistry lessons, never mix bleach with other household cleaners; with many of them, it can react and produce hazardous gases.

Maid for You

If all this talk of cleaning has exhausted you before you even start, then by all means hire a professional.

How? First, ask around among your friends and acquaintances to see if they've got anyone they would recommend. (Really good housecleaners are sometimes so prized, however, that people are reluctant to share them.)

If that fails, look under Housecleaning in your local Yellow Pages. Before hiring anyone, be sure to ask for their references, and do check them. This is, after all, someone to whom you're giving the run of your house.

How often should they come? It all depends on your budget, and your slovenliness. Could be once a day, could be once a month. But if you're hiring a maid, don't be so foolish as to start straightening up for her. (Or, increasingly, for him. In New York, for instance, many of the finest young off-Broadway actors put on a stellar performance with a chamois cloth and a bottle of Windex.)

What should you expect to pay? Rates vary, according to the work and the region of the country you're living in. But by and large, you should expect to pay around 40 or 50 dollars for a solid half day's labor. (And you'd be amazed at what a hard-working pro can accomplish in only a few hours.)

Handyman

Somewhere—don't ask me where exactly—it is written that men are handy. That they know how to fix things. That they're good with tools. That they're born knowing all about stuff such as fillister bolts, glazing compound, and soldering irons.

It ain't always so.

If you're not Bob Vila, you're going to have to overcome one major psychological obstacle before you undertake any household repair. You're going to have to recognize that every time you swing a hammer or sand a shelf you are not putting your entire manhood on the line; mistakes are inevitable, and even professionals—carpenters, plumbers, electricians—make them all the time (though they have the luxury of charging you for them).

At the same time, you must equip yourself with the basic tools you'll need to do things right. Turning a loose screw with the side of a dime, or hammering in a nail with the bottom of a heavy stapler, you're just asking for trouble. (And a new stapler.) So what are the bare essentials every toolbox should contain?

- A flashlight. (With fresh batteries.) If you can't see the problem, you can't ever fix it.
- A 10-ounce (medium weight) claw hammer. (That claw end is what you use to pry up the nails you hammered in, sideways, with the stapler.)
- Several screwdrivers. One each of the small, medium, and

large slotted kind; plus a No. 1 and No. 2 Phillips (which have those little x-shaped points).

- A ruler, and a 12-foot metal tape measure.
- Pliers. Ideally, one pair of slip-joint pliers (the standard issue) and one 7-inch needle nose pliers (for getting into those tight corners).
- An adjustable Crescent wrench (used for tightening and loosening nuts and bolts).
- Electrical tape, masking tape, string, glue, sandpaper, steel wool, stud finder, and an assortment of nails, screws, nuts, bolts, tacks, brads, etc. (The loose nails and such will lend your toolbox a very satisfying, and official, rattling noise when you carry it around.)
- Safety goggles. (Sparks, splinters, and shards can fly, while you're doing even the simplest chores.)
- A metal toolbox, in which you keep everything in its appointed slot, shelf, or compartment. What's the good of owning all these noble implements if you can't lay your hands on them when needed?

Moving On

Some things you can fix (a leaky faucet), some things you can't (the Navy airfield next door).

Sometimes it's simply time to move on.

Moving is a chore, to be sure, but one that occasionally needs to be done. Here, some tips to make it all a little less arduous:

Preliminaries

- Call up all your friends. Don't say anything about moving. Just say you're calling to see how they are, and because you care. You may need them later—particularly if one of them owns a van.

• Go to the post office and ask for one of those Change of Address kits. Get plenty of the postcards, too. Start peeling the labels off your magazines, etc., and affixing them to these cards. It's a good idea to give the post office, and other important correspondents, thirty days notice of your new address.

• Start stocking up on boxes. Any time you see a decent one—sturdy and unsullied—sitting on the curb, grab it. Check your local liquor stores—they've usually got good strong boxes lying around, too.

• Start discarding stuff. Face it—you won't be wearing that *Phantom of the Opera* T-shirt again. (And the girl who gave it to you lives in Omaha now.) When in doubt, throw it out.

• But stuff that might be of use to someone else, donate. There are many charity organizations, from the Purple Heart Veterans to local historical societies, that will come to your place, collect these things, and leave you with a healthy charitable deduction for your taxes.

• Call three movers, and have each of them send someone over to give you an estimate. Insist on an actual visit (no phone quotes), and a written estimate that is either guaranteed, or fixed to within ten percent. After you've got the three prices, factor in the other considerations (such as your gut feeling about each company) and make your choice. The cheapest course isn't always the wisest.

Packing Up

• Figure out how many boxes you think you need, then double it. If you haven't rustled them up yourself, have the moving company drop them off beforehand (assuming, that is, you plan to pack yourself).

Packing yourself is much cheaper. But having the company pack you is much easier. If you're bringing lots of expensive crystal, china, antiques, etc., the mover may insist on packing the valuable stuff you've taken out their insurance on.

• Pack with deliberation. Haste in packing will lead to endless frustration at the other end. So . . . have lots of tape, labels, and magic markers on hand. Label, or write, on each box what's inside.

• Make sure each box can be lifted without a crane. Books, for instance, weigh a ton; when you're packing 'em, fill the box half full, then use the rest of the space for lighter things.

Moving Day

• Make sure you're up and awake before the movers arrive. Get in a good shave and shower—you may be too exhausted at the end of the day to do anything more than fall in a heap. And your shower curtain may still be sealed in a box somewhere.

• Tell the movers whatever you need to tell them, then get out of their way. Good movers are like robots—efficient, thorough, concentrated. And since you're paying them by the hour, the more time they spend kibbitzing with you, the more it'll cost you in the end.

• Have some cold soft drinks on hand. Offer them to the moving men. Ideally, these soft drinks should be caffeinated and sugared. You want your workers to stay awake and energetic.

• Have a sheet with written instructions to your new address. You don't want the truck making any wrong turns. If there's anything they need to know—about one-way streets, freight elevators, back stairs—write it down.

Give this sheet to the foreman.

• In your new place, station yourself by the door and as the movers bring in each piece of furniture, tell them exactly where to put it. Once they're gone, the piano is likely to stay wherever they left it.

• Despite the high cost of moving, it is customary to tip the individual workers at the end of the move. If you moved across town, and it took the better part of a day, you should consider at least fifteen or twenty bucks to each person on the crew. Or you can give a lump sum to the foreman and let him divide it up.

Unpacking

• Start discarding all over again. Just because you brought it to your new place doesn't mean you have to keep it now. If you can't figure out what to do with it, or where to put it, toss it.

• Do not be overwhelmed (even though the mountain of boxes is overwhelming). Unpack the essentials first—your CDs can wait.

• Plug in a couple of lamps that cast a warm glow. Hang up a favorite picture or two. Make the bed. With a few small efforts like these, you can give the place a homey feel.

· Having paid a lot for the boxes, you may be determined to hang onto them for the next move. You may decide to remove all the tape, flatten them, stuff them in the closet ... but you will never use them. Six months later, you'll finally break down and throw them out.

Do it now, and save yourself the headache.

CHAPTER II

In Style

"Costly thy habit as thy purse can buy,
But not express'd in fancy; rich, not gaudy;
For the apparel oft proclaims the man."
—WILLIAM SHAKESPEARE, *Hamlet*

The Shopping News

Maybe it's a throwback to those hellish afternoons, traipsing after our mothers through the boys' department, trying on wool sport coats and corduroy pants. Or perhaps, as some anthropologists suggest, it goes back even farther, to our atavistic memories of prehistoric hunts.

Whatever the reason, clothes shopping remains, for many men, one of life's more onerous duties. But if you feel this way, there are ways to make your forays easier, more successful, and as a result, less frequent.

Your first critical decision is in the choice of store. And here, there are basically three ways to go:

• If you want lots of personal attention, and a pre-honed selection, stop in at one of those boutique or men's specialty stores. These stores come in two essential varieties: first, there's the kind of place that has catered to the landed gentry for generations: J. Press, Brooks Brothers, Paul Stuart. (Other such stores, even if they have only one outpost and it was opened last week, have similar Waspy sounding names.) If you work in a conservative profession or firm, this is a good place to go.

The other men's boutique store is the kind with startling window displays—ebony-headed, futuristic dummies, surrounded by Mylar panels—and a salesman standing by the door, ready to pounce. These stores usually have a clever name like Mano a Mano, or Machismo. When you see one of these stores coming up, cross the street.

· Another way to go is the men's section of a department store. Here, of course, you're lucky to get any help at all. You can roam the aisles for hours if need be, blissfully free of interruption; you can stand in one place for as long as it takes to figure out how much 30 percent off of $48.50 comes to. And even then you don't have to buy anything.

But if you are in the buying mood, and perhaps would welcome some assistance, think twice before selecting a salesman. Look around the selling floor—is there anyone there whose fashion advice you would trust? Do you really want to discuss cuffs with the guy whose trousers hover several inches above his ankle? No, look for the best-dressed salesman you can find—or at least the one who comes closest to sharing your own taste.

If you're unsure of your own tastes, try this helpful hint. Pick out a fully dressed mannequin you like, and then ask a salesman to replicate its outfit in your sizes. This was my favorite method when I first started working in New York; uncertain about what to wear with what, and figuring the dummies were put together correctly, I'd simply point to the one I liked and give the salesman my personal stats. Twenty minutes later I was wearing the same shirt, tie, jacket and pants, and, for the amusement of the guy doing the alterations, duplicating the dummy's pose. Tailors all over town found this, I'm sure, an inspired bit of shtick.

· Your third alternative is the cut-rate clothiers, with names like Le$$-2-Dre$$, Y Pay More?, and Discount House. According to the advertising for these places, they're filled with "designer clothing," costing far less than the department stores charge. But who are these designers— Omar of Toledo, Maurice of Anaheim? Even the worst clothing had to be designed by somebody, and most of their stuff is here. And while there might be some bargains buried somewhere in the racks, the chances of finding them are slim. Unless you really know fashion, from labels to lapels, save your time.

Finally, remember this cardinal rule: it is better to have a few items of apparel, of good quality, than closets full of stuff that screams, "I got it on sale!"

Suiting Up

Your business suit is the single most important—and costly—fashion decision you will make. It is wise to give it your undivided attention. If you've only got half an hour to spare at lunchtime, don't run out and buy a suit. There's just too much riding on it, and too many factors to take into account. You'll get a suit, all right—it just won't be the right one.

Preliminary Considerations

· What sort of suit do the other young executives at your firm wear? Even more to the point, what does your boss wear? Emulation is the sincerest form of flattery—and if you're wearing a suit that he'd approve of, you don't have to say a word about the esteem you hold him in.

Regarding style, there are so many considerations, and so many ways to go, that you must really consult your own soul, and a knowledgeable salesman. What kind of pockets, for instance, do you prefer—flap pockets (the most traditional), besoms (the imperceptible, unflapped slits), open patches (visible patch, no flap)? You alone must determine what look you feel most comfortable in—do you feel at your best in a sleek, padded-shoulder, ventless European style, or are you more the understated, rounded-shoulder, center-vented American type? If you try on a suit and you see in the mirror a man you'd trust and want to know, you're okay. If you see a guy that makes you want to hold on to your wallet and count the spoons, keep looking.

· What's missing from your wardrobe? A lightweight, summer suit, for the annual convention in Florida? A herringbone tweed, for gatherings at the company's shooting lodge? Know what it is you're looking for before you sally into the stores.

In terms of fabric, there are now hundreds to choose from—there's a mill somewhere churning out a miraculous new blend of synthetic and natural fibers every other minute. But if you want to be safe, you can never go wrong with some variation in wool—a worsted (wrinkle-resistant, and great for travel), wool crepe (drapes well, in a year-round weight), covert cloth (earthy tones, durable as armor), and trusted flannel (which is as much a part of autumn as falling leaves).

• In terms of pattern, the pinstripe is perhaps the most upscale, followed by solids and the slightly thicker chalk stripe. Unless you're in one of the "arty" professions—TV, advertising, music—you're probably better off with one of these basics, and in a color like dark blue or gray. And in a style that isn't too up-to-the-minute. (Sorry, but in most professions, boring works.)

Other patterns you may consider for business wear are:

Nailhead. Yes, it looks like thousands of tiny nailheads (hence the name), and it's got both sophistication and versatility going for it. You can wear it in the boardroom, and it still has enough pizzazz to go out to dinner in afterwards.

Houndstooth. In sport coats, the check is larger; in a suit, it's usually very small, which enables you to wear the suit almost as if it were a solid.

Glen plaid. If you've already covered the standard business bases, and you want to try something a little . . . wild, you can try this subtle plaid (also known, since the late 1800s, as the Prince of Wales plaid). The pattern is sufficiently sporty that you can wear the jacket, in your off hours, with a pair of khakis.

At the Racks

• When shopping for a suit, wear one. Not only will you get better service from the sales personnel and tailors, you'll have a useful benchmark to compare the other suits to. Do they feel as comfortable as this one? Do they fit as well?

• If you're not wearing a suit, be sure to wear at least a dress shirt, slacks, and a pair of the shoes you would normally wear with a suit. This way, when you try the suit on, the tailor can hem the pants to break the right way on the dress shoe, and he can see how long the sleeve of the jacket should be (allowing about half an inch of your cuff to show). It's also a good idea to fill the pockets of the new suit—both the trousers and jacket—with whatever you're likely to be carrying when you wear the suit. If it's bulging, or sagging, or sticking out somewhere as a result, it's better you know that now. The tailor may be able to make some allowances for it.

• If the trousers have to be taken in, or let out, more than two inches at the waist, you should seriously reconsider. Also, you should be sure you have enough room in the thighs, and in the rise (the area from the crotch to the waistband). Try sitting down, getting up, striding across the dressing room.

As for cuffs, they're generally preferred in business attire; not only do they give the suit a finished look, they also make the trousers hang straighter. Ideally, the cuffs should be an inch and a quarter to an inch and a half wide, and they should break on the top of your shoe.

• If you're wondering if your jacket is the right length for you, try standing straight with your arms at your sides, palms flat against your sides. If by curling your fingers, you can take hold of the bottom of the coat, it's correct. Too short, and you could wind up looking like Pee Wee Herman; too long, Johnny Cash.

Quality Checks

• Take the time to read that label. What's the suit made of? Its fabric and fiber content will determine how well it holds up during the course of the day. If you want to do a quick test, try the method pioneered by John T. Molloy, the man who wrote *Dress for Success*: "Grasp the sleeve of the suit jacket in both hands and twist it tightly for a few seconds . . . If the sleeve immediately springs back to shape, it's a wearable suit. If wrinkles remain . . . well, you've just wrinkled a suit you're not going to buy." Needless to say, do this while the salesman is busy helping another customer.

• Look carefully at the stitching around the pockets and buttons. Is it neat, tight? It should be. What are the buttons made of—cheap plastic, or the classier bone? How about the lining—what's it made of, and does it feel securely anchored? If not, you could find it coming loose after two or three dry cleanings. Does the suit have a pattern? If so, has it been joined seamlessly? Nothing says "cheap suit" faster than a stripe that doesn't link up, or a check that doesn't mesh.

• Are the cuff buttons functional, or just tacked on? Only the best suits have buttons that actually open and close. If you can get buttons that work, do.

• When you pick up the suit after the alterations have been made, try it on again before leaving the store. Just because they've already got it wrapped up in a plastic garment bag doesn't mean they can't take it out again. You've paid for quality (I presume)—insist that you get it.

Also, insist on getting back any swatch of material the

tailor cut off during the alterations. You'll find it's very handy to take along when you go shopping for shirts and ties to go with the suit.

Care and Maintenance

You've done everything right so far—you've bought a quality suit, in a pattern and style that becomes you—so don't let things slide now. Take care of this proud new addition to your wardrobe. That means hang it up on a curved wooden hanger as soon as you take it off (draping it over the back of the sofa just isn't the same). If it's a good suit, merely hanging it in the closet, free and clear, will allow most of the day's wrinkles to disappear.

Wielding a soft-bristled suit brush, give it the once-over to remove any dirt or city soot it picked up during the day; this grit can wear away at the fabric. Finally, check for spots or stains, and if you find them, use a spot remover to get them out. Don't rush out to the dry cleaner with it every time.

Why not? Because even the best dry cleaners have to use chemicals and mechanical presses, and none of this is good for the suit. Get it cleaned maybe two or three times a season—and if you're about to retire it for a few months, be sure to have it cleaned beforehand. Then put it in a garment bag, and wait for its season to come round again.

At Play

On your own time, away from the office, you can make your own rules about what to wear. A pith helmet and jeans? Madras shorts and clod-hoppers? Surgical scrubs? Whatever you like, as long as you don't scare the neighbors.

But do be aware that life is full of surprises. The day you're running errands in your Bill Clinton–style running shorts—the ones that so cunningly emphasize the diameter of your thighs—is sure to be the day you bump into Ms. Right at the check-out counter. The day you decide to get just one more wearing out of that old raincoat with the lining hanging out is the day you'll run into your employer, his wife, and their three perfectly groomed children. If you're going to go out among other people looking like a wreck, then go all the way and make it a proper disguise—dark glasses, large hat, possibly a wig.

Many people opt for what's known as "sweats" in their leisure hours. Loose and baggy, with drawstring belts or elasticized waistbands, and available in a veritable rainbow of unnatural hues, sweats effortlessly advertise several things— you're in lousy shape (which is why you appreciate the generous cut), you're uninterested in meeting anyone, you have inordinate trouble fastening all those buttons and buckles on normal attire. And you're color blind.

But casual wear, as opposed to more dressy apparel, does allow for a wider range of options, in style and material. Trousers, for instance, are best left uncuffed and uncreased. Shirts may sport patch pockets, short sleeves, snap buttons (though I would still draw the line at epaulettes). Footwear can range from loafers to sandals. (If you wish to be mistaken for an academic sort—or you actually are one—be sure to team up the sandals with a pair of black socks.)

Sneakers, of course, are the most popular shoe these days. But even here you might wish to exercise some caution. Certain name brands—Reebok, for instance, or Sperry Top-Siders—have an upscale, sporty cachet to them. White is still the color of preference. And as for all those fancy doodads— inflatable soles, neon heels, red velcro bindings—I think you should take a pass. Unless you're very hip, under eighteen, and can lay in a three-point shot from the mid-court line, you've lost the right to wear shoes like that.

Underwear

What you wear under all those other clothes is a very personal matter (unless you happen to be President Clinton, who, as we all learned on MTV, wears briefs).

In underpants you really have but two choices: there's briefs, those snug-fitting models with the elastic waistband, and there's boxers, the roomier shorts that come a few inches down the thigh.

Briefs provide comfort and support. They're also more likely to be what you wore growing up, so there's a certain sentimental value to wearing them.

Boxers are what your dad wore. They come in everything from cotton to silk, and in a variety of wild patterns that briefs have never been able to touch. In case it matters, they're also rumored to be a better choice if you're looking to increase your chances of fatherhood; apparently, by allowing more breathing room for the testicles, they increase the quality and quantity of the sperm production. There is also a weird hybrid known as the boxer brief: brief on top, boxer on the bottom, it has all the disadvantages of both, in one garment.

If you're considering something in the lo-rise, mesh, or g-string styles, stop it right now.

Undershirts are much more a matter of personal taste: lots of men don't wear them at all. And some wear the ribbed, sleeveless style; this is not what you'd call the power T-shirt. This is more what you'd wear while tossing pizza dough.

If you plan to wear a T-shirt, wear the short-sleeved variety, in white only, with either a crew or V-necked collar. If you wear a tie most of the time, you should wear the crew, as it will make less of a visible impression through your shirt. If you wear an open-collared shirt, wear the V-neck, and make sure that you don't open so many buttons that the top of the T-shirt shows. As a rule of thumb, never open more than one button below your collar button—unless, of course, you teach a mambo class in a Florida strip mall.

Finally, change your underwear often—and not because you might get hit by a car and taken to the hospital (if that happens, the last thing you'll be worrying about is your underwear). No, change it often because it's the grown-up and proper thing to do. And because your mother would be proud of you.

Tying One On

"It is universally allowed that the least constraint of the body has a corresponding effect on the mind," wrote Emile Marc de Saint Hilaire, one of Balzac's buddies, "and it must, therefore, be admitted that to a certain extent a tight Cravat will cramp the imagination and, as it were, suffocate the thoughts."

Maybe that's why you fall asleep at the office.

But the necktie is still, as Saint Hilaire also called it, a man's "letter of introduction," and as such, some care must be taken in its selection. It speaks even before you do. (So do you really want it to say, "Hey, I think wearing something that's got Daffy Duck all over it is pretty darn clever"? Probably not.) Among the more traditional tie patterns, there are several from which you may safely choose.

• Solid ties are certainly safe, but also breathtakingly boring. (Solid white, however, is good only for a Mafia wedding, and solid black for a funeral.)

• The rep, or regimental rep, tie is one of the most conservative. Diagonal stripes, generally in dark colors, it's been a proud part of the business uniform for time immemorial.

• The Ivy League tie, with a pattern of small diamonds or circles, is always acceptable. So is the club tie, with heraldic shields or some other repeating motif, such as golf clubs or mallards.

• The polka dot is okay, though beware of any dots larger than a pencil eraser. The smaller the dots, the more professional the tie.

• The paisley, those amoebalike shapes swimming in a sea of color, is very hit-or-miss. Some are beautiful, and their swirl of colors can artfully pull together the other elements of your ensemble. Others are muddy or too bold. So be careful with these, unless you have a good eye.

In respect to fabric, silk is top of the line. And a silk foulard is the most elegant tie of all—lightweight, sleek, and correspondingly expensive. But even a regular weave silk tie should have a subtle shine—without glistening—and take a knot well.

Ties made from a silk and polyester blend can pass muster, but only if the silk plays the lead role and the polyester is content to provide durability. If the tie glows like the sun at noon, forget it.

Ties in wool, and wool knits, are sometimes bulky. So if you're a big man to begin with, with a large face, you might want to avoid these altogether, as they will only make you seem even more stolid. Before buying one, try it on to see that the knot doesn't look too large, that the fabric doesn't bunch under your collar, and that after it's tied you've still got enough tie left over to hang the right length.

What *is* the right length? Most ties are cut to a 56″ length, which should provide plenty of hang for any man under 6′6″. (Beyond that, it may be time to head for the Big and Tall Shop.) To get the maximum length, tie a four-in-hand knot, or a half-Windsor—they use up less material.

Whatever the knot, the two lengths of a properly tied tie should be almost even, with the underside just a little bit shorter. Since tie clasps are no longer in style, it's okay to keep the bottom strip from straying by slipping it through the band sewn to the back of the tie. The bottom of the tie should just graze your belt buckle, or waistband. (If you're not wearing pants with your tie, we need to talk.)

Knotty Problems

There's more than one way to tie a tie. But four of the most popular methods, ranging from the four-in-hand (the most appropriate knot for conservative dress) to the ascot (appropriate for garden parties, yachting adventures, and anyone with an arty bent), are described and diagrammed below. They are shown as they would appear in a mirror.

Clip-ons are not an option.

The Four-In-Hand

1. Begin with the wide end of the tie hanging down on your right, and about twelve inches or so longer than the narrow end.

2. Cross the wide end over the narrow end, and bring it back underneath the narrow end.

3. Keep on going—bring the wide end across the front of the narrow end one more time . . .

4. . . . then pass the wide end up through the loop at the top.

5. With one finger holding the knot in place, push the wide end of the tie down through the loop in front.

6. Gently tighten the knot, then draw it up to the collar by holding on to the narrow end and sliding the knot up. You want it neat and in place, you don't want it to choke you.

The Half-Windsor

 1. You start out the same way as with the four-in-hand—the wide end on your right, hanging about a foot longer than the narrow end.

 2. Step 2 is the same, too—cross the wide end over the narrow end, and then back underneath it.

 3. Here's the switch—now you bring the wide end up and turn it down through the top loop.

 4. Pass the wide end around the front from left to right.

 5. Then pull it up through the loop . . .

 6. . . . and down through the knot in front. Gently pull the knot up to your collar.

The Bow Tie

 1. Begin with the end in your left hand hanging about an inch and a half lower than that in your right hand.

 2. Cross the longer end over the shorter, then pass it up through the loop.

 3. To make the front loop of what will be your bow (if all goes according to plan), double over the shorter end and position it across your collar points.

 4. While you use the thumb and forefinger of your left hand to hold the loop, let the long end of the tie flop down over the front.

 5. Putting your right forefinger, pointed up, on the bottom half of the part that's hanging down, pass that part up—behind the front loop—and . . .

 6. . . . poke the resulting loop through the knot (behind the front loop). Even up the ends, tighten it, and you're ready to party (if it hasn't already ended).

The Ascot

1. Start with the right end hanging about six inches below the left.

2. Cross the right end over the left, then bring it back underneath.

3. Cross the right end around the left end one more time.

4. Now pass the right end up through the loop at the neck.

5. Let the right end flop down over the left end.

6. Fluff the bib at the top, so that it covers the knot. Leave the collar of your shirt open, and tuck the points of the ascot into your shirt.

Whatever the knot you're tying, do untie it when you get home again. If you leave the knot in, you run the risk of permanently wrinkling the fabric. The best method of removing a tie is to reverse the steps you took to tie it.

Finishing Touches

It's those little touches that can dress up any outfit—or, if done wrong, undermine it. Herewith, twenty-five nifty tips to successful accessorizing.

· The width of your tie should correspond to the width of your lapel—wide lapel, fat tie; narrow lapel, skinny tie.

· You should always carry a fresh handkerchief—and it should always be made of white linen or cotton. Anything else is wrong for both showin' and blowin'.

· Never wear a shirt that is darker than your suit or sport coat. Never wear a tie that is lighter than your shirt.

· Shirts that have a contrasting collar look dandyish and finicky.

· Bow ties work well if (a) you are playing Clarence Darrow in summer stock, (b) you are teaching classics at Boston Latin, or (c) you have a button in your pocket that will make the tie squirt when you press it. In all other cases, think very hard about why you're wearing this.

· If you still insist on the bow tie, wear it with a button-down shirt; both have a certain sportiness about them.

· There is no such thing as a short-sleeved dress shirt; if it's a dress shirt, it's got full sleeves. If it's got short sleeves, don't wear it to work, or any other important occasion.

• A good dress shirt should have no pockets. But as most of them are made with one pocket now, that's become acceptable. Two pockets, no. Flaps on the pockets, no. Snaps—do I have to keep repeating myself?

• Socks, especially those you wear to the office, should be dark and over the calf. If they sag, if they allow even an inch of your bony shank to show when you cross your legs, you have evinced a wanton disregard for everyone around you.

• Trenchcoats must be beige. Black, blue, olive, gray, you name it, are all reserved for cops—in Eastern Europe—and guys who think that beige is boring. (These same guys think mirrored sunglasses are cool.)

• Mirrored sunglasses are not cool.

• You should always carry a slim, expensive-looking pen, especially to meetings where you might be trying to sell something to someone. A leaky Bic can do you in faster than an attack of Tourette's.

• The standard wallet, the kind that fits in your back pocket, is fine—if it's a dark leather. What's known as the "pocket secretary" billfold—longer, larger, the kind that will fit only in the pocket of a suit jacket—has a kind of continental savoir faire about it. But whichever you carry, it shouldn't be so crammed with credit cards, receipts, cash, etc., that it squats in your pocket like a hamster.

• If you carry a briefcase or attache, it should also be made of dark leather—brown, preferably. It should not have lots of hardware on it, combination locks, straps, clamps, etc. You do not want to look like you're about to embark on an episode of *Mission Impossible*. And those aluminum briefcases? I guess if you work for the National Institutes of Health,

you could come up with some excuse for carrying one—
you're transporting live viral specimens?—but if not . . .

• Cuff links should be worn, of course, with formal
wear, but otherwise very seldom. On the Count of Monte
Cristo, they looked good; on you, they're likely to look . . .
foppish. Still, if you must, stick to small, simple links, in gold
or silver; if they include stones, the stones should be real.

• Monograms—on shirt pockets, handkerchiefs, whatever—are the kind of touch that people without class think is
classy.

• Jewelry on men, like furs, is a matter of taste: if you
have taste, you'll know better. A man should wear a handsome wristwatch, an unobtrusive ring if he chooses, a wedding band if he's married, and that's it. Neck chains are for
those guys who dive off the cliffs in Acapulco, and bracelets
belong on Barbie.

• A novelty wristwatch is fun, amusing, and best worn
away from work. After everyone has seen how Elvis glows in
the dark, they will fast lose interest.

• A belt, properly sized, will fit comfortably on the
third notch. The buckle should never be overly large or shiny,
nor should it carry your initial. (See "Monograms," above.) It
shouldn't be much wider than an inch, and its color should
match your shoes.

• Collar pins, stickpins, tie clasps, and tie bars are all
best seen at the track.

• Money clips go well with stickpins.

• An umbrella should be black, with a simple wooden
handle. While the fold-up kind has certainly become acceptable, the old-fashioned, uncollapsible variety has much

greater cachet. Golf umbrellas, colored umbrellas, and umbrellas that carry the name of the cologne you had to buy to get the umbrella as a free gift are distinctly downscale.

• Eighty percent of your body heat escapes through your head. Or maybe it's ninety. Who can remember? Who cares? A hat, of course, will keep that from happening. It will also cast your face into shadow, blow off into the street, and carve shapes into your hair that would put topiary artists to shame. If you still want to wear a hat, make it one of the standard models—a classic Fedora, for instance—and understand that everyone who sees you in it will know you're going bald.

• The baseball cap—and please wear it with the brim *forward*—is popular now for weekend wear. Understand that everyone who sees you in it will know you're going bald.

• Eyeglass lenses should be clear or, if not, tinted only slightly. Contacts should always be clear; wear colored, and you're liable to look like an outtake from *The Man Who Fell to Earth*.

Eyeglass frames should complement the size and shape of your face, and your complexion; bring someone you trust to the optician with you. Since you'll be effectively blind during the try-ons, listen for auditory clues. If your friend is chuckling, guffawing, or calling up your other friends on the pay phone to "Get over here quick—you've got to see this!" you should try a different pair.

Black Tie

If you're over 21 years of age, you have stopped growing. (Vertically, at least.) And if you have entered into the normal course of civilized life, you will have occasion, now and again, to attend black tie affairs. Social events, charity balls, business-related wingdings—you'll notice them cropping up more and more often. And each time, you will have to decide whether to rent, or buy, the formal wear required.

Renting a tuxedo is relatively less expensive—a hundred bucks, say, instead of six hundred or so to buy. But let's do the math here—rent six times and you might just as well just have bought the damn thing. Other advantages to the outright purchase plan? The tuxedo will fit better, it will be available at a moment's notice, and you won't have to race back the next day to avoid paying a late charge.

When you do decide to take the plunge and buy, ignore all fads. You want your tuxedo (or, dinner jacket) to look correct and presentable for many years to come, so even if they're wearing foot-wide lapels, or Nehru suits, on the streets at the time, you want to steer clear. You can opt for a single-breasted jacket with a notch lapel, a double-breasted jacket with a peaked lapel, or a shawl collar with a rounded lapel, but whatever you do, keep it dull.

"Dull," you say? Yes. Black tie affairs guarantee everyone in attendance that two things will happen: the men will all look alike, so nobody has to give them a second glance, and the women, by comparison, will stand out all the more in their finery. (Why do you think women generally organize these things?)

Your tuxedo must be black. And it's best to buy it in a light weight. One thing you can count on at black-tie affairs is central heating.

Your shirt must be white: furthermore, your shirt must be flat, or pleated. No ruffles. Of the two traditional collar shapes, the wing collar is the more formal (this is the kind that sticks up like something in a Charles Dickens movie), and it's the one that does the most for men with long, thin necks. The turned-down collar, on the other hand, is more comfortable and less conspicuous.

Your bow tie must be black; its fabric should relate to the fabric of your lapels—satin to satin, for instance, or twill to grosgrain. While the kind you actually tie yourself is best, a bowtie that has a ribbon that runs all the way around your collar and fastens in back is okay. Clip-ons are not.

Your suspenders must be black, your vest (or cummerbund) must be black.

Your shoes must be black—either lace-up black patent, or patent leather pumps with grosgrain bows. Your socks must be black, sheer, and rise above your calf.

Your jewelry—shirt studs and cufflinks—should be discreet, subtle, and (ideally) of a matching pattern.

Are you angry with me? Do you think I'm a killjoy? If you feel that you really must assert your individuality, you may certainly do so—you can wear a red pocket square, or bow tie. You can put on Mickey Mouse suspenders. Or a colorful vest. Or replace the black shoes with white Nikes. It's a free country, and you can express yourself however you like. I'm just telling you how it's *customarily* done.

But if you really feel that the topaz string tie is *you* . . .

Best Foot Forward

There was one good thing you could say about bell bottoms—they hung down so low, you never had to worry about what shoes you were wearing. Who could see 'em?

Well, these days your shoes do show. So you have to pay attention.

In general, the heft of your shoes should roughly correlate with the weight of the garments you're wearing. In other words, you don't wear a feathery leather slip-on with a heavy Harris tweed sport coat. Try a wing tip, instead.

Depending on the business you're in, you might be able to get away with a pair of fancy loafers. But by and large, business attire looks best with conservative, lace-up shoes. (Which also happen to lend more support to your feet.) Wing tips, cap toes, plain toes, oxfords—in well-polished, unscuffed leather, they all look good.

As for color, black, worn with dark blues and grays, is your safest choice. But there are other colors you can try. A cordovan can go well with a navy suit, a brown can lend some interest to a gray ensemble. What you should avoid are shoes in more than one color, and shoes in unnatural colors (which means any hue you've never seen leather take on before).

Also, avoid boots—and even worse, those little half-boots—unless you work in very close proximity to cows.

Because good shoes are expensive, it behooves you to take care of the ones you've got. Should I talk about shoe trees? I know, I know, you've heard about them before, you've seen them for sale in the shoe store, you even found one once in your parents' attic, but they really do help to preserve the life of your shoes. A good, wooden (cedar, in particular) shoe tree helps to hold the shape of the shoe, and at the same time absorbs leftover moisture. You can buy them in your own shoe size, or you can get the adjustable kind that's now on the market. Any time your foot isn't in the shoe, the shoe tree should be.

Another way to get longer wear out of your shoes is to alternate them. No, I don't mean put them on the wrong feet: I mean wear a different pair the next day. And never dry them by sitting them, wet, on top of a radiator.

In respect to polishing your shoes, there are two ways to

go about it: the do-it-yourself, and the professional. The do-it-yourself method requires that you get a clean rag and wipe off any dust or grit on the shoe. Then apply saddle soap. To put on the color, use a paste wax, rather than a liquid, and let it dry, unmolested. Take a brush, or a nappy cloth, and give the shoe a brisk rubbing, then give it an equally brisk buffing with a soft rag or cloth.

For a few dollars, however, you can save yourself all of this elbow grease, and go to a professional shoe shiner. (They are still found in barber shops, at train stations and bus terminals, and at random spots on city streets.) For many men, I am well aware, there is something vaguely stuffy about this, something suspiciously undemocratic—they feel foolish, sitting there reading the stock tables while some poor schnook labors over their feet. But you really should get over this (the shoe shine guy has). He'll do a much better job than you will, and if your conscience still bothers you, you can give him a fiver.

The Kindest Cut

Barbershops are not only good places to get your shoes shined—they're also good places to get your hair cut.

Yes, there are styling salons, where men and women are both welcome. Where they have a cappuccino machine in the waiting area. Where Kenny G. is playing softly in the background. Where you're a whole lot more likely to find a copy of *Mirabella* than *Playboy* lying around.

And if you like your hair styled and moussed and gelled, this is where you should go.

In a barbershop, you'll find barbers—men (and occasionally women) who cut hair for a living, and are proud of it. They don't know who's editing *Vogue* these days, and they don't care. If they go by only one name, it ain't Antoine—it's Dwayne.

When looking for a new barber, ask around among your friends—particularly among those whose hair looks good.

(Ideally, you should have your hair cut about once a month. During the summer months, however, it tends to grow a little faster.)

Once you've plunked yourself down in a barber's chair, tell him what you want. And be as specific as possible. Don't just say "medium on the sides," if what you want is for the hair to just graze the top of your ear. If that's how you want it, say so. Barbers aren't mind readers.

If you want a more natural look in the back, ask him to use only scissors, not an electric razor.

If you like a very short cut, consider carefully the shape of your skull. Is it nicely rounded? Or more like a watermelon lying on its side? Longer hair can conceal a multitude of problems.

At the same time, don't drive the barber crazy with constant instructions. Give him his marching orders, then relax and let him do his job.

Assuming he does it well, you should tip him ten or fifteen percent of the cost of the haircut. Unlike stylists, who have somehow managed to convince the public that their services should cost about the same per session as a psychiatrist (Is it because one of them works on the inside of the head, and the other one on the outside? Is that the logic?), barbers usually charge somewhere between eight and fifteen bucks.

Finally, you must remember that barbers prize loyalty above all other virtues. If you go to someone else, and then come back the next time, don't ask him to give you a shave. You don't want to put a razor in his hand.

Pressing Matters

How much is it costing you to get your shirts cleaned and pressed? How many times have they come back missing a button? Or with a stain you don't remember putting there? Finally, how much time have you got on your hands? Depending on your answers to these questions, you will, or will not, be interested in the instructions that follow. To wit, how to iron a shirt.

First, the iron. You will notice it has different settings for different materials. Probably acrylic and acetate at one end, linen at the other. Check the label in the collar of your shirt, then turn to the matching setting. With me so far? Good.

Now it gets harder. What are you ironing on? A kitchen table, covered with a towel? A countertop? An old bathroom door, supported by two sawhorses? Get an ironing board. And, if it's a dress shirt and you like that semi-stiff look, a bottle of spray starch. Otherwise, a spray bottle filled with water will do. Before running the hot iron over any part of the shirt, give the cloth a spritz with your bottle. Pretend you're aiming a gun; play Shane.

Okay, now it's time to put the metal to the material. We'll start by ironing the back of the shirt. Open it up and place it face down across the square end of the board. Smooth the fabric out with your hand, give it that spritz we spoke of, then . . . iron. Run the iron over the cloth in even, uninterrupted strokes. When you've finished with the area on the board, reposition the shirt by pulling it until the other side seam snuggles up against the side of the board, and then iron this area, too. If there's a center pleat, not uncommon on dress shirts, don't panic. Just run the pointed end of the iron into and under the sides of the pleat; then flattening the pleat out, iron it down completely. Fear not: when you wear the shirt, that pleat'll pop right up like it's supposed to.

Okay. On to the front. Turn the shirt over, and lay it so that one half is facing up on the board, while the other trails off toward the floor. This side, I'll admit, is kind of scary; you've got pockets and buttons to deal with, not to mention that if you leave a scorch mark, the shirt is a dead loss; you can't even get away with wearing it under a jacket. So go slow; don't let the tip of the iron catch under a button, or grind over it. As for the pocket, iron it from below; that way the iron won't accidentally snag the fabric and tear it.

All right, what's left? The sleeves and the collar. Lay one sleeve at a time on the board; iron the front of it, all the way down to the cuff (watch those buttons!), then do the back. As for the collar, you'll never be able to get this to lie flat—it's just not made that way—so do your best. With the shirt facing up, open the collar and run the iron across its entire length. Then remove the shirt from the board, put it on a hanger, and start with the next one. (You didn't really go to all this trouble to iron one shirt, did you? Do a few at once—maybe even a pair of pants—'cause we both know it'll be a cold day in hell before you wrestle that ironing board out of the closet again.)

The Confidence Game

No matter how well-dressed and pressed you are, you're really not ready to go out in public until you have just one more thing, that invisible but indispensable element known, these days, as self-esteem.

If you don't feel good about yourself, if you don't feel entitled to walk the earth among your fellow men, if your self-confidence is at ground zero and falling, it won't matter how impeccably your suit is cut, or how brightly your shoes shine. You'll radiate defeat and sorrow.

Short of going in for intensive psychotherapy, or a course of artificial mood elevators, there are a few things you can do, easily and inexpensively, to lift your spirits and boost your confidence. You can:

Take action. The last thing you want to do when you're feeling useless and ineffective is to do something. But the best thing you can do is to force yourself. Even if it's only cleaning out the closet, or reconciling your bank statement, you'll get a small sense of accomplishment from having completed the task. Any task.

Get physical. If, perchance, there's something physically taxing you can do—such as shoveling the walk, or raking the leaves—so much the better. Physical exertion decreases the muscle tension caused by anxiety, and at the same time releases some helpful neurotransmitters (such as serotonin and dopamine) in the brain. If there's a pickup basketball game you can join, do it.

Call your friends. I know, I know, when you're feeling down on yourself, the natural inclination is to hole up in your burrow. But getting out among people, especially people who like you, is the best possible tonic. The very fact that you have these wonderful friends may, on some level, help to persuade you that you are indeed likeable—and that you, too, should start liking yourself.

Smarten yourself up. True, that impeccably cut suit won't solve your problems, but looking good—getting a haircut, putting on something colorful and fun—can help. People respond to you more favorably when you look your best, which in turn raises your self-esteem.

Fake yourself out. If you're frowning, stop it. If your facial muscles are instead configured in a smile, your brain gets the message that you're feeling happy. Treat yourself to something you've wanted to buy, or do something you've been longing to do. Pretend you feel better about yourself, and your prospects, than you actually do. Before long, the make-believe will start to shade over into reality.

CHAPTER III

In the Pink

*"Early to rise and early to bed makes a male
healthy and wealthy and dead."*

—JAMES THURBER,
Fables for Our Time (1940)

What's on Top

Growing up, you never gave your hair much thought. When it was long, you got it cut. When you were going out, you ran a comb through it. About your hair, you were fairly cavalier.

But with age comes wisdom—and now you know that your hair may not always be with you. Just look at what's lying around on the bathroom counter, or clogging the shower drain. And what was that you spotted in the department store's three-way mirror—a glint of light off the back of your head, where the overhead beam caught a thinly veiled patch of scalp?

Shudder.

If you want to make the most of your hair while you

have it, and take what steps you can to ensure that it sticks around as long as you do, here's how.

Cleansing

You walk into your friendly drugstore or supermarket, you scan the shelves of shampoos and conditioners, and you just want to go back to pouring a flat beer over your head and whishing around the lather. How can they make this many things just to pour on the top of your head?

Take solace in this: detergent and water. That's really what all these different concoctions are made of. Much of the rest—the herbs and thickeners, honey and balsam and vitamins—is chiefly designed to give one product or another an advertising edge. And most of these "special ingredients," like the rest of the stuff, just runs right down the drain, anyway.

What you want is a simple, inexpensive shampoo that, from trial and error, seems about right for your hair. That means you should be able to use it once a day without finding that your hair lies flat as a mackerel or fluffy as cotton candy.

That said, the general shampoo categories you will encounter (and you won't learn *this* in any college classroom) are these:

• Daily shampoos. A little lower on the detergent scale, a little higher on the moisturizer side. For most folks, these do the trick.

• Moisturizing shampoos. They're meant to leave the hair's natural oils relatively unmolested. Made for dry, brittle hair, they're usually loaded up with humectants (stuff such as amino acids and glycerin).

• Body-building shampoos. Lower on oils and moisturizing ingredients, they're correspondingly heavy on proteins and polymers, whose purpose in life is to coat the shafts of your hair and add thickness.

· Shampoo-and-conditioner combos. The general consensus, among hair-care professionals, is that these don't clean as well as regular shampoos, or condition as well as separate conditioners. But for ease and speed, they're tops.

· Conditioners. Oy—you see how easy it is to get sucked into all this? There are a zillion different conditioners, for hair that's dry, oily, matted, greasy, tangled, treated, fine, atomically altered, you name it. You can try one or two of these, and if you like the way it leaves your hair—after you've applied it according to the instructions on the bottle—go ahead and use it, once or twice a week.

How to Shampoo

Very simple.

First, wet your hair thoroughly.

Then, massage a small amount of shampoo into your hair, using your fingertips. Gently work up a lather.

Rinse off said lather with a gentle spray (we don't ever want to hurt our hair in any way we can avoid), and make sure you get all of it out. If you don't, your hair can be left looking dull. The harder, and more mineral-laden, your water is, the longer you'll have to stand there under the spray.

Even if your shampoo label recommends lathering all over again, forget it. That's just a ploy to get you to use the stuff up sooner. Do it right once, and you're done.

If you find that your hair is "squeaky clean" most of the time, you may be overdoing it. Some Sunday when you won't be seeing anyone, give it a day off.

And once in a while, switch shampoos. Hair appreciates variety, too.

Scalp Trouble

Dandruff, seborrheic dermatitis, psoriasis—such an unlovely triumvirate.

Dandruff, the most common scalp ailment, can be caused or exacerbated by many things—stress, illness, seasonal changes (usually it's worst in winter), oily shampoos, genetic predisposition.

Seborrheic dermatitis (crusty, itchy patches on the scalp) most often afflicts people with oily skin and hair.

Psoriasis, the result of excess skin cells on the scalp (and elsewhere) that become scaly and inflamed, is often chronic, and probably hereditary.

What do you do about them? First, get your dermatologist to confirm for you which one you've got. Then you can try one of the therapeutic shampoos designed to treat the problem. These shampoos contain one or more of six FDA-approved ingredients: zinc pyrithione, selenium sulfide, coal tar extract, sulfur, salicylic acid, and a combination of those last two.

In most cases, for dandruff you'll want shampoos containing zinc pyrithione, sulfur, salicylic acid, or selenium sulfide.

For seborrheic dermatitis and psoriasis, you should look for coal tars (though if your hair is light in color, check the label to make sure this shampoo has been formulated not to discolor light hair).

Preventive Measures

To stave off these problems before they start, or if you've already had a run-in with one of them:

- Don't shower in very hot water. This can just dry out your scalp all the more.
- Don't rub your scalp too much when shampooing, or brush your hair more than necessary.
- Use a hairbrush with soft, rounded bristles.
- Lighten up on the blow dryer. Let your hair dry naturally.
- If you've got a hat on, and you can feel the itching or sweating start, take the hat off.
- If the air in your home or office is noticeably dry, run a humidifier.

Brushing Up

Consider the humble hairbrush. Every day you grab it off the bathroom counter—but do you really look at it? You whisk it a couple of times through your hair—but do you really pay attention? You toss it back and head out the door—and leave your hairbrush lying in the dark, on a damp spot next to the toothbrush glass.

It deserves better than that.

Your hairbrush is one of your most important grooming tools, and as a result you should give some thought to the kind of brush you use, and just how you use it. Let's start out by pointing out some of what your brush does for your hair and scalp.

For one thing, your hair takes a beating these days. The ozone's shot, the air is so polluted you have to part it with your hands, the shampoos and conditioners you use leave all kinds of chemicals and residue stuck to your follicles and scalp. Your brush is the best friend you've got when it comes to undoing the damage.

A good brush will not only clean the hair, but stimulate the scalp below, which in turn improves the flow of blood to the roots of the hair. At the base of each hair, there's a tiny gland that produces sebum—Mother Nature's own conditioning oil. Every time you run your brush through your locks, you distribute this sebum all along the length of the hair, making the hair more supple and giving it a healthy sheen. At the same time, you bring out the color of the hair, too.

To accomplish all this marvelous stuff, however, you need a decent brush—not some plastic paddle you fished out of the dollar-ninety-eight bin. The bristles of a good brush must be hard enough to penetrate down to and stimulate the scalp, and soft enough not to smart. The better hairbrushes, such as those made by the venerable English firm of Mason Pearson, are made out of the natural bristles of the wild boar. (For all the animal-rights activists among you, the boars are reputedly unharmed by the collection of the bristles.) In each tuft of boar bristle, there's also one rounded strand of nylon, a bit longer than the bristles, to make sure the scalp gets tickled.

If you have normal to fine hair, you'll probably want to use a pure bristle brush. If your hair is very fine, or even—how should I put this?—thinning, you may want to go soft. For thicker hair, you may want to try the mixed bristle. If what you have is a veritable mane, something Chewbacca might be proud of, you will probably have to resort to a heavier nylon component.

Finally, if your brush is going to keep on doing its job, you have to take care of it. Never apply a mousse or styling gel to the brush itself. To clean it, wash it in a warm solution of water and mild soap. (No detergent, no ammonia.) Rinse it very well, then put it on a towel to dry, with the bristles down; this will allow air to circulate through it. Let it dry, naturally, for at least a day. (While you're waiting, use your spare brush, or just don't go out.)

The Bald Truth

If there's any comfort to be had from this dismal affliction, it's that men who go bald are men who are positively deluged with the male hormone, testosterone. Barry Diller, Dwight Eisenhower, Michael Milken—all, in their own way, achievers.

No comfort, huh?

Okay, here are a few things you can try when you start to notice your own hair is looking a little sparse. (The notorious comb-over—letting the hair grow long on one side, so it can be flopped over to cover the top—is not one of them.)

• Minoxidil-based solutions, such as Upjohn's Rogaine. First, you've got to see your doctor to get a prescription. He can tell you exactly what you're getting into. For one thing, the stuff currently will run you about sixty dollars per month. For life. If you stop using it, you can expect to lose much of the hair growth it stimulated.

Also, it works best early on—at the first signs of hair loss. Even then, it only works in some cases, and not at all in others. It will take at least several months of use before you know if you're one of the lucky ones or not.

A clear, non-oily liquid that is applied directly to the scalp, Rogaine can also produce some side effects, including irritation and a red, itchy scalp.

• Hair transplants. Now they can do mini- and even micro-grafts, gathering up little patches of skin and hair from spots where the follicles are still healthy, and transplanting them to spots where they're not. This doesn't come cheap, however; it requires the work of a surgeon skilled in this sort of thing, and your bill, depending on how many grafts are done, will run several thousand dollars for sure. To find a surgeon with transplant experience, you can call the American Hair Loss Council (1-800-274-8717), the American Academy of Facial Plastic and Reconstructive Surgery (1-800-332-FACE), or the American Society for Dermatologic Surgery (1-800-441-2737).

• Toupees and hairpieces. If you do decide to take this route, get a really good one. Even the best toupees are usually spottable, and the worst can render you an unwitting object of fun. Drive a used car if you must, live in a trailer park, wear discount clothing, but don't try to economize on a hairpiece. Get one that matches your natural hair color, and that doesn't make too dramatic a statement (no one will believe that Fabio mane).

Close Shaves

Although in some ways this is the most dangerous thing you do all day—holding a razor to your own throat—you think nothing of it. You do it when you're half awake, with your vision still bleary, while you're listening to the news and weather reports. You give it about as much deliberation as you do pulling on your socks.

Perhaps it's time to reconsider.

A wise shaving regimen is one that gets the job done, as quickly and comfortably as possible, and at the same time does the least damage to your face. Those two aims are not mutually exclusive—in fact, if you're following a few basic principles, and using the right products, you'll find that a smooth shave is also a smart one.

The Preparation

· Wake up. Have some coffee. Leave the dream state. You want your eyes to be wide open and your brain in gear before you start.

· Do you shave before showering, so you can rinse off all the lather in the shower stall? Start shaving after showering; this will give your skin a chance to absorb some steam and moisture, after the long and drying night. The mirror's fogged? Wipe off a section with a towel.

· If you still insist on shaving first thing, at least give your face a thorough dousing in warm—not hot—water. Or soak a washcloth in warm water, and hold it on your face for a minute or two. You might also use the cloth to give your face a gentle massage, softening up the skin and raising the beard.

· What kind of shaving cream are you using? Is it the can with the 79-cent sticker on it? What a deal. But be advised, there are a host of shaving creams and gels on the market now, which may be a help if you're suffering from anything like razor burn, bumps, cuts, etc. Loaded with stuff such as glycerin, aloe vera, and almond oil, these products can really soften up a beard and caress the skin beneath.

If you haven't tried any of these radical innovations, ask yourself why. Is it the money? The cost differential isn't that great—and where are you gonna get another face if this one wears out? Are you afraid you'll smell like perfume or something afterwards? Forget it—when you rinse off the stuff, the

smell goes with it. Do you think the whole thing is just too
. . . fussy? (Read "feminine.") Hey, it's not a beauty product
you're buying—it's a shaving product. If you still have a
problem, buy from a place called Kiehl's. Not only do they
manufacture some of the best men's products around—such
as their Ultimate Brushless Shave Cream, or Blue Astringent
Herbal Lotion—the stuff comes in very functional-looking
bottles and tubes. And the store, at 109 Third Avenue in New
York, even has motorcycles on the selling floor. There—now
are you happy?

The Shave

• Whatever the shave cream you elect to use, let it sit on
your face for a minute or two before you start scraping it off.
Give it time to soak into your bristles (though not so much
time that it starts to dry out).

• Use this minute to consider your razor. When you
shaved yesterday, did it drag? *Now* is the time to change the
blade—not after "just one more shave."

Is it a disposable razor? Dispose of it—forever. You
might as well be using an old butter knife as one of these
flimsy plastic doodads.

The Gillette Sensor, one of several on the market (and
my own personal favorite), is sensibly priced, and good with
a moderate to rough beard.

• Shave *with* the grain of the beard; shave against it and
you'll instantly know, from the blood, the pain, and the
ingrown hairs that result. Generally, your shaving strokes
should be in keeping with the dictates of Mr. Gravity—
downward.

Unless you hope for a career like Jim Carrey's, don't

pull at your face and attempt to move the features around. Mr. Gravity is going to take care of that, too, for you—and sooner than you know. Just leave the landmarks right where they are, and maneuver the razor instead.

The Aftermath

• Your skin is freshly exfoliated—a nice way of saying you've scraped off a layer of skin—and now it's ready for a little pampering.

What you don't want to recreate is that scene from *Home Alone*—Macauley Culkin was right, aftershave can sting.

If the brand you're using smarts, it should follow that disposable razor—right into the wastebasket.

Nor should you start slapping on fragrance. Those alcohol-based scents should be kept in reserve; later on, when your skin can stand it and the object of your affections is close enough to be struck dumb by the pheromone attack, you can apply a dab or two.

• Rub your lower face, gently, with a moisturizer or toner laden with good things such as camphor, or clove, or that old standby, aloe vera. What you're doing here is making peace with the portion of yourself you just attacked. Do you really want to go out into the world with your face complaining about you? I don't think so.

• Throughout the day, use the occasional moisturizer not only to keep your skin soft and supple, but to make shaving the next day that much easier. Many skin care products, such as the new Lift Off! series from Aramis, also offer sun protection; as side benefits go, that's a darn good one. (According to company research, "Men spend 38 percent more time in the sun than women and so their risks of getting skin cancer are higher.")

• Sleep in a humidified room—it'll keep your skin from drying out—and before retiring for the night, apply some moisturizer again. It won't come off on the pillows, and it will leave your face prepared for the next day's onslaught.

Addendum: Facial Hair

But wait, you may say to yourself. Couldn't I save myself an immense amount of time and trouble simply by growing a beard or a mustache? Wouldn't I then be able to spring out of bed in the morning, and get to work ten minutes earlier, thereby impressing the boss with my punctuality and verve?

In a word, no. (And this comes from one who tried it.) The boss wasn't impressed, women weren't bowled over, and the extra ten minutes disappeared into the great cosmic yawn.

Some hard facts that must be faced: beards and mustaches are extremely tricky items. Wearing them well is more difficult, and even more time-consuming, than going close-shaven.

For one thing, any man can shave himself. But trimming a beard is much like cutting your own hair—a maddening exercise in which you keep on trying to even things up until you have a patchy furze that only a team of specialists with an electron microscope can repair. Trimming a mustache, though easier, still requires a deft touch, sharp scissors, a close-up mirror, and patience.

The downside is also far more dangerous than anything that can occur with a close-shaven face: a five o'clock shadow never caught a gluey strand of egg drop soup. If you elect to wear facial hair, you must consult restaurant menus with great care and foresight. Most Italian food is out; ribs are impossible; even fried chicken can prove hazardous. When they wheel the pastry cart around, remember that an errant pastry flake from that tempting Napoleon can insinuate itself into your thatch in the batting of an eye, and accompany you proudly into your next meeting.

Stick to coffee and cake.

But if you are still bound and determined to wear a beard or mustache, if you feel your weak chin needs the camouflage, or your cheeks demand the warming ground cover, keep several things in mind: even in today's most enlightened business surroundings, facial hair must be impeccably maintained and of a fairly conservative style if it's going to pass muster. In other words, a devilish goatee or a sweeping handlebar mustache are going to draw more notice than is wise. Keep your beard close to the contours of your face (in other words, no Santa Claus stuff), and your mustache likewise.

If you like the idea of sideburns, make sure they are cut evenly across the bottom, and extend to the same point of both ears—ideally, no more than midway. Below that, and you'll look like you belong in a rockabilly band. Bushy and full sideburns, also known as mutton chops, should never be worn outside of a Civil War battlefield—where, presumably, you work as a tour guide.

Smile

Of all the shocks that flesh is heir to, one of the most common, and least photogenic, is gum disease. Three-fourths of American men will suffer through at least one bout with it.

What can you do to improve your chances of giving gum disease—and the dreaded root canal—a miss?

You can—dare I say it?—learn to brush properly.

I know, I know, you've been hearing this stuff for years from parents, teachers, and nubile dental hygienists (and why *are* they all so good-looking?), but have you ever really listened?

Right here—and if you pay attention, you'll never have to sit through all this again—is a quick and handy guide to oral hygiene and dental preservation.

• Brush your teeth at least twice a day. If you haven't been brushing twice a day, this, more than anything else, may explain why you live alone.

There really are bacteria in your mouth (it's not just toothpaste-commercial hype) and they really do team up with a gummy substance called mucopolysaccharide to build plaque; plaque, in turn, calcifies and turns into tartar. This is not stuff you want in your mouth. Brushing and rinsing can get some of it out.

Though there are many theories of proper brush use, the consensus now is that you should brush at a forty-five-degree angle to the tooth. But whatever stroke you use—horizontal, circular, a mixture of both—just do it. Gently, and for two minutes each time you brush. And brush everything, from those back teeth you never see, to the tongue you can't miss. The tongue? Yep. Once a day brush your tongue to get rid of bacteria, and to improve your breath.

• What kind of brush should you use? Again, different styles have come in and out of favor. But currently, most dentists are recommending a soft bristle. And for once, synthetic beats natural (natural can accommodate bacteria too easily). Every few months, when you notice that the bristles have flattened out like a wheat field in a windstorm, get a new one.

• Toothpaste. According to the American Dental Association's Council on Dental Therapeutics, no toothpaste sold in the U.S. has ever actually been proven to combat the bacteria linked to gum disease and plaque. What about all those claims, on all those tubes? If you use one of those miracle-bearing toothpastes, you probably won't be doing yourself any harm, but you probably won't be doing yourself any special good either.

Toothpaste serves three functions really: it acts as a lubricant while you swab your toothbrush around, it gently abrades the food grit still clinging to your teeth, and it can (if it is so composed) introduce fluoride to your mouth—and fluoride is still the only drug recognized by the FDA and the ADA to fight tooth decay.

• Flossing. You knew I'd bring this up, didn't you? It's such a nuisance. If you do it while watching TV, you risk flinging microscopic food particles around the room. If you do it in front of the bathroom mirror (which also allows you to see what you're doing), you could die of boredom. To make this nightly chore go more smoothly, find a floss that doesn't catch or shred in your teeth. There are waxed, unwaxed, tapes, ribbons, you name it. My wife swears by a product called Glide (made by the same folks who bring you Gore-Tex).

There are also, for the record, some gizmos that claim to do the flossing for you. One, the Oral Ease Automatic Flosser & Power Brush, has a tiny flywheel that whirls the floss around at thirty-five revolutions per minute (for $99). Panasonic makes another, the Power Floss and Brush, which features a choice of brushing motions, speeds, and flossing stems ($116).

• See your dentist every six months (more often if you have some ongoing problems). You laugh when I say this; like, who doesn't know to make an appointment when you get that little reminder postcard? But fifty percent of the American population doesn't. Go, and let that lovely young hygienist (And why is it always a different one? Where do they all go?) scrape away that nasty tartar from under your gums and off your teeth. She wants to do this for you—let her enjoy herself, while you lie back and try not to dribble too unbecomingly.

A Breath of Fresh Air

"Bad breath," the bane of modern life and a boon to advertisers everywhere, has many different causes. Among them are:

• smoking and/or chewing tobacco
• drinking alcohol
• gum disease
• respiratory tract infections
• aromatic compounds—found in such foods as garlic and onions—that enter the bloodstream, get carried to the lungs, and then are exhaled.

If you take the usual measures—brushing, flossing, etc.—you've done most of what you can do to combat bad breath.

If you use a mouthwash, understand that most of them do a better job of masking the problem than they do of solving it. And even their masking abilities wear off in anywhere from a few minutes to an hour.

As far as their plaque-fighting powers go, the most powerful is something called Peridex, a prescription-only rinse with the American Dental Association's Seal of Approval. Good at reducing plaque and gingivitis (swollen and inflamed gums), it has its drawbacks: it tastes bitter, it stains the teeth brown (though your hygienist can get the stain off again), and it's not cheap (about $20 for a 16-ounce bottle).

Listerine, the old standby, was, up until a few years ago, the only nonprescription rinse with the ADA anti-plaque seal. But Listerine—known to those who can't tolerate its mouthburn as "Blisterine"—also has a high alcohol content, and some recent studies by the National Cancer Institute have linked alcohol to a slightly higher incidence of mouth and throat cancers. So it's something to think about.

In a six-month study, Viadent rinse, when it was used in conjunction with Viadent toothpaste, also reduced plaque and gingivitis.

There are, of course, a host of other mouthwashes on the market—Scope, Cepacol, Lavoris, Colgate Fluorigard, you name it—and all have their virtues and their drawbacks. Which one should you choose? Chiefly, it's a matter of taste, because if you don't think it tastes good, you won't get around to using it at all.

The Sun Also Braises

Remember your parents turning off the TV and telling you, "It's a sunny day—go outside and play"? Remember how you thought it was for your own good?

So did they.

But now, of course, a bunch of spoilsport medical researchers have mustered all sorts of evidence to show that sunburns in early life, from infancy through the teen years, increase the chances of contracting skin cancer in later life. And the national melanoma rate, according to the American Cancer Society, has been rising by four percent every year since 1973.

(See—you were right all along. You *would* have been better off staying indoors, watching those *Brady Bunch* reruns.)

Anyway, it's not too late now to make up for all those hours in the great outdoors. To protect yourself against further exposure to those harmful UV rays, you can:

• Apply a sunscreen, or sunblock, every day. But be aware, there is a difference between the two.

Sunscreens contain special ingredients whose sole purpose is to absorb and neutralize ultraviolet radiation. The potency of sunscreens is measured in something called the SPF (Sun Protection Factor). What you want is one that measures 15 or stronger, and that protects against both UV and UV-B rays. (UV-B rays, which comprise only about 5 percent of the ultraviolet radiation that makes it to earth, can also be very potent cancer-causing agents.)

Sunblocks, on the other hand, repel all UV radiation, through the use of ingredients such as titanium dioxide and zinc oxide. These ingredients also manage to block out the infrared light, or "heat" rays, of the sun; some doctors think these rays are more responsible for skin damage than we know. While sunblocks can offer a lot of protection, their efficacy can't be measured in the same way as sunscreens, so they don't carry SPF ratings.

• Stay indoors between 10 A.M. and 3 P.M., when the sun is at its strongest. And remember that temperature has little correlation with sun risks: UV radiation can be strong even on a cool and cloudy afternoon.

• If you must be out in the sun, wear clothes that have a tight weave (never wear a mesh T-shirt, anyway, under any circumstances) and, if you have the guts, don a hat with a wide brim.

• If you're planning to swim, slather yourself with a waterproof sunscreen. If you're wearing one of those newly popular sunless tanning lotions (they've now come up with some products that don't turn your skin yellow or orange), remember that most of them offer little or no UV protection. In other words, even though you look tanned, you've still got to put on something to keep from getting burned.

If, even with all these precautions, you still manage to get a sunburn, soak the affected portion of your anatomy in cold (not ice) water for a quarter hour or so. Or apply a cold compress. A coating of aloe vera will also provide some relief. Aspirin, ibuprofen, or other anti-inflammatory drugs may help; so might hydrocortisone cream. For all-over sunburns, try submerging yourself in a tub of water into which you've added one cup of dry instant oatmeal. (Really.)

If you've actually reached the stage where you've got blisters, congratulations—you've acquired a *second*-degree sunburn. If the pain persists for a day or more, you may need to visit your friendly dermatologist—who will tell you all the things that I just have (but charge you a lot more).

Addendum: The Mole Story

What I'm about to suggest is no fun, but necessary. One of the early warning signs of skin cancer is a mole that's visibly changing. The American Cancer Society recommends that adults check their skin once a month: one way to make this task more pleasant is to check someone else's. Thoroughly. And then have her return the favor.

Since people who have atypical moles are more likely to get melanoma, here's a quick rundown—the "A, B, C, D" of moles, as it were—to tell you what to look for:

A is for asymmetry. Do the two sides of the mole not match up?
B is for border. Is the border irregular or blurred?
C is for color. Do parts of the mole show different colors, shades of tan, brown, black, or even—patriotically—red, white, or blue?
D is for diameter. Is the mole larger than the eraser on a pencil?

If you've got a mole that shows any of these signs, or if you've got one that's changing on you, walk it in to your dermatologist for a look-see.

Back Talk

Despite all the attention you pay to your front—is your hair combed? tummy flat? fly zipped?—it's your back that can really do you in. When your back goes out, everything goes with it—from your sunny disposition to your camping trip in the Ozarks.

So what can you do about it?

Back pain is one of the most common afflictions that God decreed Mankind should suffer. (Only childbirth is a more popular reason for admission to a hospital.) If your back pain is chronic, severe, or impinging on your daily life, hie thee to thy doctor. If it radiates into your buttocks and limbs, if it's causing any loss of bowel or bladder control, or if your legs are feeling wobbly or numb, hie thee there double-quick (if you can hie at all).

In the meantime, to relieve routine strain on your back and to keep your vertebrae neatly aligned, try to incorporate the following into your everyday life:

• Bend at the knees. When you have to pick something up, don't double over from the waist—bend over, bring the object in close to your chest, and then slowly rise.

• Squat. For power lifting, and for necessary chores like looking to see what's in the back of the bottom shelf of the fridge, squat down on your haunches, keeping your back straight. Sure, you might split your pants now and then—but maybe that'll keep you out of the fridge so much.

• Lose some weight, if you're carrying around more of it than you should. The best way to go about it is with exercises that strengthen your hip flexor, abdominal and thigh muscles; all of these muscles can help to alleviate pressure on the spine, and keep back problems from popping up again later.

• Carry your wallet in your breast or front pocket—not the rear of your trousers. Sitting on it all day throws your posture off and puts pressure on your spine. A friend of mine, who's been hospitalized twice for back problems, now carries a money clip, instead of a wallet, in his side pocket.

• Ask for help. Just because you bought a new air conditioner, that doesn't mean you have to carry it out to the car—at the far end of the parking lot—all by yourself. Tell the salesman you'll need some help; if you still find this embarrassing, tell him an old injury is acting up, from your days as a Navy Seal in 'Nam.

• Stop being gallant. A little old lady is struggling to get her steamer trunk out to the cabstand? Don't lift a finger. Lift a hand, instead, to help her summon a porter.

• Get up from your chair every so often. Sitting in one position for prolonged periods of time is bad for your back. Don't slouch or slump.

• Before you sit down again, try placing a back pillow, or lumbar cushion, on the seat.

• Get a firm mattress—and sleep on it. Do not sleep on a sofa, a sofa bed, or, God forbid, a hammock. When getting up, do it in stages—roll over to the side of the bed, swing your legs to the floor, straighten up, and arise, slowly.

• Don't sleep on your stomach; you can imagine what this does to your spine all night, bending it like a drawn bow. Two better sleep positions are (a) on your back, with a small pillow under your head and a larger one under your knees, or (b) on your side, with a pillow under your head, one cradled under your top arm, and another between your knees. Okay, okay, so this isn't exactly studlike, but it is much better for your back. Think of all those pillows as belonging not to a nerd, but a pasha!

Gym Dandy

You think you're doing the right thing—you're exercising. Working up a sweat. Sticking to a regular workout schedule.

But wait—you are also exposing yourself to a host of

microbial invaders, particularly if you're using a less than hygienic health club. Look around the place—have you ever seen a mop wielded in the locker room? Are there black streaks around the air vents? (Where are they drawing their air from—a coal mine?) Do the windows actually open? (Even in an urban area, the air trapped inside the place is likely to contain more pollutants than the air outside—this according to a number of EPA reports.)

When choosing where to exercise, pick a place that's open and airy, where the ceilings are high and the windows can be opened, where the towels are picked up from the floor, the exercise machines are wiped down after each user, where standing water is promptly mopped up, and the temperature and bacteria levels in the hot tub are regularly checked. (Pseudomonas bacteria, which can cause an irritation of the hair follicles, can stay alive even in fairly hot water; this irritation, known as folliculitis, usually clears up on its own, but if it doesn't, you may have to resort to a regimen of antibiotics.)

If you should succumb to one of the more common gym-related complaints, here's what to do:

If what you've got is athlete's foot, take some comfort in numbers—by last count, 26.5 million other Americans had a problem with it, too. It's caused by tinea, a persistent little fungal agent that just loves moisture and sweat; given a choice between Paris in the springtime and the space between your toes, tinea will go straight for the toes every time. Once there, it creates an unpleasant red rash, peeling skin and itchy fissures.

Your best defense against athlete's foot is to not catch it in the first place: wear clogs around the locker room and showers. In fact, keep two pairs in your locker, so one pair can dry out while you wear the other. The clogs will also protect you from the ubiquitous papillomaviruses, which cause those unsightly and painful plantar warts.

Make sure your feet are kept clean—put on fresh socks after each sweaty workout—and dry: after you wash your feet, towel them off well, and sprinkle talcum or anti-fungal foot powder between the toes. Lotions aren't as wise an idea; they add moisture, which is just what you don't want.

Once athlete's foot has erupted, there are several different topical sprays and creams you can try, including Naftin, Micatin, Tinactin, and Mycelex. Most of these will eradicate the rash in a few weeks—though it's important to keep using them for a while even after your feet are feeling better. The rash could unexpectedly pop up again.

It can also pop up elsewhere—in your crotch, for instance, where it's responsible for the dreaded jock itch. Again, prevention is the best defense: don't wear the same workout clothes twice in a row, don't hang out in a wet bathing suit, don't wear synthetic, bikini-style underwear (stick to loose cotton, changed daily), and if you've already had a problem with athlete's foot, put your socks on before you pull up your underwear—that way, you won't risk transferring the fungus from one place to another.

To treat jock itch, you can apply many of the same antifungal agents as are used for athlete's foot, but if it becomes a chronic problem you may want to bring in some bigger guns—stuff like ketoconazole or griseofulvin. Check with your doctor, for the appropriate pronunciation.

These last two medications, administered in oral doses, are also used to treat fungal infections of the toenail (and fingernail, if you're foolish enough to scratch your feet). The affected patch turns a whitish yellow color, and the nail can become thick and soggy. To ward off nail fungus, you should keep your feet clean and dry (lots of fresh socks), and to fight it you should employ a fungal tincture, or apply a mix of thymol and chloroform directly under the nail. To make sure the medication gets where it's supposed to, scrub the nailbed at least once a day.

Against all of the above, take swift and sure retaliation—otherwise they'll just spread and prosper. If the over-the-counter remedies don't work, do not consult the guy on the next StairMaster (what does he know?), or your girlfriend (she'll act sympathetic, but trust me, she'll be privately appalled). Consult your doctor.

Toe to Toe

If the only time you think about cutting your toenails is (a) after you've gouged a hole in your bedmate's leg, or (b) after you've sliced clear through the front of your Nike, it's time to think anew.

Cutting your toenails should be a regular part of your personal hygiene regimen. Whenever your toenails grow to the end of your toe, it's time to cut them. If they're normally hard and brittle, you might consider cutting them after you've taken a hot shower (which can soften 'em up a bit).

The best method is to use toenail clippers, and to clip in a straight line across the toe. If you attempt to angle your cut into the corners, you run the risk of cutting too deep, and incurring the dreaded ingrown toenail.

If you do wind up with an ingrown problem, daub some antibiotic ointment on the infected edge of the toe and cover the salve with a Band-Aid to keep it from being wiped away. An ointment can lessen the pain, fight the infection, and soften the nail somewhat (so it doesn't burrow into your skin quite so effectively).

Walking Tall

If you haven't heard by now, yes, walking is now considered one of the best, most effective, and least dangerous forms of exercise. Take a leisurely stroll, for only one mile, and you'll burn up 100 calories; turn up your speedometer to four miles per hour (not exactly a killing pace) and you'll burn up 352 calories; another notch—to four and a half miles per hour—and the calorie burn soars to 428.

All this, and the greatest danger is that you'll trip over a crack in the sidewalk.

Walking not only lowers your weight, but improves aerobic capacity, reduces your cholesterol, alleviates stress, tones your muscles, and lifts your spirits (it's prescribed for many patients suffering from depression).

Brisk walking—also known as power walking—does all of these in spades. To get the most out of your own walks, you might try:

• Walking tall. Stop looking for coins on the sidewalk—what's the big deal about a dime?—and start keeping your head up, eyes straight ahead. Don't slouch.

• Pump your arms, elbows tucked in close to your sides. Use your arms to set your pace—the faster you pump them, the faster your legs will go. Work those upper body muscles as you walk.

• Lean forward slightly. If your arms are pumping in front of you, this will be your natural posture.

• Take deep, regular breaths.

• Contract your abdominal muscles. Since their everyday job is to keep your torso stabilized while you get around, they'll get a serious workout from a power walk.

• If you want to pick up your speed, take shorter, quicker strides. With each step, concentrate on pushing off the ball of your rear foot; this will exercise your glutes and hamstrings.

Clearly, you shouldn't try any of this until you've put on a good pair of walking shoes. Shoes that are durable, flexible, and relatively new; once you've worn the heel away, it's time to toss them. If you're planning to walk around on sidewalks, take a pass on sneakers with lots of groovy treads and bumps on the sole—these can catch on cracks in the pavement.

To make your walks more interesting, vary your route, and wear headphones. As for the music you listen to, you might be wise to choose upbeat, faster-paced stuff. It's tough to break a sweat while listening to Pachelbel's *Canon*.

No Sweat

Sure, you want to work up a sweat when you exercise. But what you don't want to do is to become dehydrated. By the time you get thirsty, you're already 1 to 2 percent dehydrated.

So how can you keep your exercises on schedule and your water levels up?

Prehydrate yourself thoroughly ten or fifteen minutes before your workout. That means drinking 10 to 15 ounces of fluid—water or juice. Avoid alcohol and caffeine—both of them will only dehydrate you further.

Drink some more fluids after twenty or thirty minutes of exercise.

Do your exercising in a cool, shady place if possible; avoid open concrete lots, blacktop, beaches, and direct sunlight. If you are going to be in the sun, wear a hat or visor, sunglasses that filter out UV-A and UV-B rays, and a sunscreen with an SPF of at least 15.

Wear loose, light-colored clothing (no matter how great you look in the skintight black spandex).

Skip the salt tablets. There's no scientific proof, so far, that they help.

Stop exercising at the first sign of dizziness or nausea. Also stop exercising if you experience a dry mouth or skin, or if you get the chills. Drink something, rest, and if you still don't feel better, see a doctor.

Paternity News

We've all heard of the deprivations and hardships prospective mothers must undergo. No smoking, no alcohol, no caffeine. But guess what? If you're planning on becoming a father anytime soon, you'd be well advised to make a few signal changes yourself. (If you haven't stopped dating around, now's the time.)

You also want to make sure your own sperm count is as high as possible, and that the ones you're producing are healthy little buggers. For instance, did you know that sperm produced in spring and fall are better swimmers than most (and consequently, more likely to fertilize an egg)? Were you aware that sperm production, like most things, falls off in summertime (probably slowed by those hot summer temperatures)? Well, now you are.

To improve your own chances of fatherhood, there are several things that you can, and should, do:

1. Cut out the cigarettes. As a display of solidarity with your mate, this will earn you lots of extra points. And overall, you're crazy to be smoking, anyway—especially when you consider that men who smoke within a year before the conception of their child raise the child's risk of contracting leukemia or certain cancers. Another study showed that babies with fathers who smoked over a pack a day had twice as high a chance of being born with a cleft lip or a heart defect.

According to studies on the effects of secondhand smoke, if you smoke after the child is born, you run the risk of slowing your child's intellectual development.

2. Raise your vitamin C intake. Some biochemical research points to a link between vitamin C deficiency and an increased level of birth defects, childhood illnesses, and other problems. Although the U.S. RDA of 60 mg a day is generally considered sufficient, men with infertility problems are sometimes helped by an increased dosage.

3. Steer clear of workplace hazards. This not only means staying out of the way of the loaded forklift—it also means giving a wide berth to toxic chemicals and radiation sources. According to studies done at McGill University in Montreal, there are over 50 industrial, medical, and other

chemicals that can adversely affect sperm, lower their count, or even cause genetic defects in children. If you've got questions about certain chemicals present in your own workplace, you can get answers by calling the National Institute for Occupational Safety and Health (NIOSH) at 800-356-4674.

Some research also has shown that there is a higher rate of defective sperm among men who work outdoors during the summer months.

4. In the bedroom itself, read the label on any sexual lubricant you and your wife may be using. Many of them contain, as a sort of bonus, a potent spermicide. Needless to say, you'll need to find another lubricant.

And give it time: don't assume you have some kind of problem if she doesn't get pregnant right away. If your wife has a regular menstrual schedule, and you have intercourse every other day, you'll have covered every day of her cycle after about three months. But many couples take longer than that to get pregnant. If you've been at it, unsuccessfully, for a year, then it might be time to investigate further, to see if there's really some undiscovered problem standing in the way.

Stress Savers

The expressway was bumper-to-bumper for thirteen miles. The meeting ran two hours overtime. You just got a letter from the IRS, casually mentioning that you've been selected for an audit.

Stress—it's everywhere you want to be, and some places you don't. Sometimes you feel so wired, it's as if you could provide enough current for a medium-sized city; other times you feel so beaten down you can't even muster enough energy to flick on the remote control.

What's the solution? Short of winning the state lottery and using the money to buy a Hawaiian island (where you'd probably wind up worrying about the next hurricane), you can lower your stress level in several ways:

• Aerobic shock. Instead of lying down and brooding about your bad day, get up and jog, swim, skate, rollerblade, walk (briskly).

• Conversely, slow down—use deep breathing and chanting techniques to achieve a state of inner peace.

• Brew up some chamomile or valerian root tea. (They're sold in those health food stores, where you always see the wan, pallid people going in and out.) They're herbal relaxants.

• Reduce your sugar, caffeine, and alcohol intake.

• Turn off the ring on your phone. Let the answering machine collect your messages for a while.

• Laugh. Rent a funny movie, go to a comedy club, call up a friend who usually makes you laugh.

• Get a massage. From a real, licensed masseur or masseuse.

• Have sex. Done right, with someone you love and trust, it can provide both physical and emotional release.

Done wrong, with someone who carries a riding crop and insists that you call her "Ms. Domina, Mistress of the Dungeon," it may have quite the opposite effect.

Heading for Trouble

The fact that headaches are among the most common afflictions—90 percent of the American population claims to suffer from them—doesn't make them any easier to take.

But some things do improve your odds of avoiding headaches in the first place—and getting rid of them sooner when they do strike. A brief rundown on the main types of headaches you can get, and how to alleviate the pain, goes as follows:

The tension (or muscular contraction) headache, the most common of all, is brought on by stress, fatigue, and sometimes just poor posture. It results in a dull, constant throbbing.

REMEDIES: Lots of over-the-counter medications can work, ranging from aspirin to acetaminophen or ibuprofen. Some antidepressants also help. Heat, or ice packs. A relaxing bath or shower.

Migraine headaches, which afflict only about 17 percent of women and 5 percent of men, can be caused by anything from sleep deprivation to certain foods. The pain is extreme, usually focused on one side of the head, and can last for days.

REMEDIES: A new drug, sumatriptan, shows great results so far. So do other medications, such as Sinequan, available only by prescription.

Cluster headaches, though fairly rare, create a blinding, sharp pain, usually centered around one eye, and can go on, in waves, for weeks or even months at a time. Men are five or six times more likely to get them than women.

REMEDIES: Various prescription medicines, including anti-depressants, have been known to work. Some patients find that breathing pure oxygen helps.

Exertional headaches are brought on by a range of things, from strenuous sex to athletic endeavors. Men are more prone to get them than women. These headaches can be very short—less than a minute—or go on for a couple of hours.

REMEDIES: Sometimes exercising for shorter periods of time can keep them at bay; at other times, a prescription painkiller called Indocin can help.

Overall, there are a number of common headache triggers, which include:

Stress
Poor or irregular sleep patterns
Changes in the weather (migraine sufferers are sensitive
   to the charged atoms in the air)
Alcohol (particularly red wine and brandy)
Food with nitrites (such as hot dogs, salami, bologna)
Chocolate
Hunger (from crash dieting or skipped meals)

Caffeine (though this can sometimes lessen headache pain, too)

Tobacco (cluster headaches are more common among smokers)

Eyestrain (bright light can sometimes trigger a migraine)

Altitude (take it easy if you go on a mountain hike)

Headache medicines (take 'em too often, and your body can come to rely upon analgesics to feel normal; when it doesn't get them, it can complain by generating what's called a "rebound headache")

Most headaches are just that—an ache in the head, soon gone and sooner forgotten. But if the pain you get is chronic or excruciating, or if you have other symptoms such as fever, nausea, weakness, confusion, blurred vision, or stiff neck, get thee to a doctor.

For information in the meantime, you can call the National Headache Foundation at 1-800-843-2256.

Eating Your Vitamins

The debate rages on: Are vitamin tablets worth it? How many should you take? In what dosage? Does it matter if they're "natural," or artificially formulated? Do they really cut down on colds? Can they stop cancer in its tracks?

Today's answers will undoubtedly be challenged tomorrow.

So what *is* it safe to say? It's safe to say that our bodies do need vitamins (for everything from energy metabolism to bone maintenance), and that the body can't manufacture them on its own. Most multivitamin tablets deliver what they claim (the Recommended Daily Allowance), but you never know how fresh or well preserved the tablets are (do check the label date) or how well these particular capsules will disintegrate, and consequently deliver their vitamin charge to your body.

Which brings us right back to the best, and most basic, vitamin delivery system of all—a balanced diet.

Here's a quick rundown on the vitamins you need, what you need them for, and how to ingest them the old-fashioned way:

Vitamin A. It's essential for normal growth and reproduction, as well as healthy skin, hair, and mucous membranes.

To GET IT: eat vegetables and fruits of the deep yellow, orange, and dark green sort, such as carrots, broccoli, spinach, sweet potatoes, and cantaloupe. Also, eat liver, if you can stand it. Cheese, milk, and fortified margarines are sources, too.

Vitamin B1 (*thiamin*). It helps prevent fatigue and irritability, while keeping the nerves, muscles, and heart healthy.

To GET IT: eat nuts, sunflower seeds, whole grains, dried beans and peas, and pork.

Vitamin B2 (*riboflavin*). Necessary for normal cell growth, it's also important to maintaining good vision and an energy-producing metabolism.

To GET IT: eat liver and other organ meats (though not on a date), or poultry, fish, cheese. Also dried fruits, leafy greens, whole grains, milk, eggs, yogurt, and nori seaweed.

Vitamin B3 (niacin). Great for healthy skin and digestive tract tissue, it stimulates circulation, too.

TO GET IT: eat liver (is this getting redundant?), other organ meats, veal, pork, poultry, dried fruits and beans, leafy greens, whole grains, milk, and eggs.

Pantothenic acid. This one supports the important work of the adrenal glands, which produce the hormones, which in turn help to counteract stress.

TO GET IT: consume nuts, beans, seeds, dark green leafy veggies, poultry, dried fruit, and milk.

Vitamin B6. You need it to make your red blood cells and to help your body use protein to build body tissue.

TO GET IT: eat bananas, dried fruit, sunflower seeds, beans, poultry, liver, nuts, and leafy green vegetables.

Vitamin B12. Also essential to the formation of red blood cells, this vitamin helps to keep the nervous system functioning smoothly.

TO GET IT: eat animal protein foods, including fish, shellfish, meat, poultry, milk, yogurt, and eggs.

Vitamin C. It stimulates the immune system, helps wounds to heal, and aids in the absorption of iron.

TO GET IT: eat citrus fruits, melons, berries, cauliflower, tomatoes, cabbage, potatoes, red and green peppers, and dark green veggies.

Vitamin D. This one helps to regulate both calcium metabolism and bone calcification.

TO GET IT: eat tuna, salmon, and cod liver oil (right), along with fortified and full-fat dairy products.

Vitamin E. Want to prevent cell membrane damage? This one does it.

TO GET IT: consume vegetable oils and their products, as well as nuts, seeds, fish, wheat germ, whole-grain products, and leafy green veggies.

Vitamin K. Though this one doesn't get much press, it's necessary for normal blood clotting.

TO GET IT: eat cabbage, cauliflower, and dark green leafy vegetables.

The Magnificent Five

Five servings a day of fresh fruits and vegetables—that, according to the National Cancer Institute, is the minimum you're supposed to get.

But how? Who has the time (or the inclination) to down all that healthful stuff—particularly in a world filled with Dove bars, spareribs, and beef fajitas?

The secret, my friend, is to remember that that's a *total* of five servings—and a serving can come in many sizes. If we're talking about fruit juice, you can down three-quarters of a cup (the amount you find in the smallest can size) and you've got one serving.

If we're talking about a box of, say, frozen spinach, eat a mound slightly larger than a golf ball, and there you've got another.

Eat an apple, or any other normal-sized piece of fruit, and another serving is accounted for.

Pick up one of those little (1½ ounce) boxes of raisins, and there's one more.

Have a salad, with a healthy-sized handful of greens in it, and that's a serving.

Other painless ways of introducing fruits and veggies into your otherwise dismal diet:

Garnish your frozen pizza with mushrooms, green peppers, spinach.

Make a baked potato, then make it edible by adding yogurt or low-fat cottage cheese instead of sour cream.

Whip up a batch of pancakes, with bananas or berries tossed into the batter. Then top off the stack with even more fruit.

Eat cereal, with fruit on top.

Have a V-8 instead of a Coke. (It's rather like a Bloody Mary, without the kick.)

If you're fixing an omelette, fold in some onions, green peppers, or tomatoes.

When preparing a sandwich, wedge some lettuce, celery, or tomatoes in between the salami and provolone.

Snack on dried fruit (a six-ounce package equals one serving).

Toss some frozen yogurt and fresh fruit into a blender and make a fruit smoothie.

Keep lots of tempting fresh produce around the house. If it's there, you'll eat it.

Hard as this may be to believe, in time these healthful foods will come to seem a natural part of your diet.

CHAPTER IV

At Work

———⊱✦⊰———

"You will never know a man till you do business with him."

—SCOTTISH PROVERB

The Job Interview

Studies show that life is unfair. Good-looking people are more readily asked to draw up a chair at the banquet of life—so do your best to be good-looking when you go for a job interview. If you're blessed by nature, good for you. If you're not, do the best with the material at hand.

Attire? Clean, well-pressed, and unless you're auditioning to play bass in a heavy metal band, conservative. You can always show off your fashion flair later. Right now you don't want a crimson pocket square to distract from your message.

Your message is you. Call to confirm your appointment, and need I mention that you should get there on time? Being late doesn't prove how much in demand you are—it just shows that you can't tell time.

Give a firm handshake, keep your shoulders back, your jaw set (an open mouth, unless it's talking, is always a worrisome sight), and walk tall. Sit that way, too—squarely in the chair.

Eye contact—maintain it, but don't overdo it. So many authorities have stressed the importance of eye contact that at least one personnel director I spoke to said that he's interviewed people who steadfastly refuse ever to look away. "It's like interviewing an owl," he says, with a shudder.

You don't ever want to make the interviewer shudder.

Do your homework. Read up on the company ahead of time, so that if you have to ask what exactly they do there, you can at least make your question more specific. ("I know you build weapons of mass destruction, but how many of these are sold to private homeowners?")

Be prepared to answer some inevitable questions:

(1) "What are your hobbies?" Even if you're about as active as a tree stump, mention something that requires standing up, moving, or leaving the house. Golf, tennis, and polo are all good, *upscale* choices. Bowling and NASCAR rallies are not.

(2) "What are your salary requirements?" A sucker's game, if ever there was one. But you will be required to play. Do everything possible, even if it means throwing a coughing fit, to get them to mention a figure first. Then, even if their figure makes your toes secretly curl with delight, keep a straight face, and say you'll have to think about that. Or move right on to the question of benefits and perks. If you must name a price, be realistic—figure out what it is, then add on fifty percent. There is no agony greater than naming your price and having them instantly capitulate. It means they got a bargain, and you got less than you're worth.

(3) "What would you say is your worst fault?" Now is not the time to tell them about your pyromania or deep-seated urge to remove the current head of state. Offer a modest smile and say something like, "I don't know when to quit—show me a problem, and gosh darn it, I'll stay up all night if that's what it takes to get it fixed." They'll know, of course, that you're lying through your teeth, but they'll respect you for sidestepping their lame little trap.

The Resume

Your whole life? On one lousy page? Impossible, you may think: What about that science fair prize? Or the year you spent in Tibet, finding yourself? Or the fact that you've won your Rotisserie league baseball for three seasons in a row?

One page.

No more.

It's an advertisement for your life—it's not your biography. And the people who have to read it are notoriously impatient.

Also, persnickety. Make sure that your one-pager is meticulously typed, and unless you're quite sure of yourself, have it carefully proofread by someone who got an A-plus in grammar, punctuation, and spelling. You might even consider having your resume done by one of those professional resume services (though even then you'd better check it over).

If there are huge gaps in your employment history—those years you were unjustly accused and imprisoned by a benighted third-world regime, for instance—consider stretching the jobs you held before and after your confinement, to cover as much of the time as you reasonably can.

For other gaps, you can always claim—though this throws up a red flag—that you were self-employed.

Massage the truth, where necessary and expedient, but do not tell blatant, and eminently catchable, lies. If you say you were one of the top-producing salesmen at your last company, that's tough to check. If you say you occupied The Blumenthal Chair in Bioengineering at Harvard, that's easy. One call to Boston, and your cloning career can grind to an abrupt halt.

The Business Card

Such a small thing, really—a slip of paper with your name and number on it. Job title, too, if you've already got one. But even if you're not gainfully employed at the moment, make the investment and order some cards with your home phone and address on them.

Why?

Because it's the simplest, smoothest way of leaving that information with anyone you might want to leave it with. Would you really rather start fumbling for a pen and scrawling on a wet napkin?

But take note—no matter how witty or artistic you are, your business card is not the place to show off your talents. Do not get fancy when it comes to the design. No splashy colors, no cute graphics, no photos in the upper right-hand corner. And no catchy sell-lines: "You've tried the rest, now try the best!" (unless, of course, you do indeed run a pizzeria). Keep it subtle, restrained, and, in size, 3½″ by 2″. Those are the standard dimensions, and with anything else you run the risk that people will have trouble stashing it away in their own wallet or card case. And don't you want to make it as easy as possible for them to preserve and protect it? You do.

Your card is also a useful item to attach to clippings, reports, and other miscellany you may be forwarding to a business acquaintance. When doing so, it's customary to jot a few words on the card—something like "Thought you'd like to see this"—and sign your first name. If you've enjoyed a dinner at someone's home and you're sending flowers to the hostess, you may also enclose your card, and write a few words of thanks on the back.

What you don't want to do, however, is distribute your cards like confetti the minute you enter any gathering. By and large, the time to offer your card is at the conclusion of the meeting or event. Never press your card on someone senior in rank to you; wait till they ask for one. Nor should you try to exchange cards with anyone at a dinner table while the meal is in progress. The idea, in almost every instance, is to make the offering of your card a personal and discreet operation; the person getting it should feel he's being given something special and valuable, not some handout on the street.

On the Line

Some business is done in person these days, some of it by mail, but a whole lot of it—possibly most—is done on the phone. Reach out and sell someone. Consequently, phone etiquette—how you make your calls, and how you take them—can prove to be vitally important to your professional advancement.

Don't get hung up by something so basic.

Making Calls

When you call a client or customer, don't just say to the secretary, "Hi. Is Beverly there?" This will inevitably call for,

"May I tell her who's calling?" Now you look pushy, and not terribly professional. Always say your own name, and if this is a call you're returning, mention that.

Be nice to the secretary or assistant. If this person comes to dislike you, you will never get through again. Ask the assistant's name, note it down, and use it in future whenever you call.

When you do get Beverly on the line, get to the point. Chitchat is fine, but during business hours people need to know why you're calling and what's up. And if you get a reputation for hanging forever on the line, folks like Beverly will start purposely avoiding your calls.

No matter how well the call goes, end it in an upbeat fashion. If you sign off glumly with a "Well, maybe next time you'll see it my way," what do you really think the chances are that she will?

If the assistant has simply told you that Beverly is unavailable, leave your number—even if you know she's already got it (why make her go to the trouble of looking it up?)—and if you can explain it briefly, say why you were calling. That way, if Beverly should call back when you're away, she can still leave you an answer of some sort.

If you get Beverly's voice mail, speak clearly, and if you're leaving some important information that has to be accurately jotted down, repeat it, slowly.

Taking Calls

If you want to know what kind of reception people are getting when they call you at the office, disguise your voice and call in yourself. (Or ask a friend to try it.) How is the person who picks up identifying your number? Is he saying

"Mr. Clark's line," or "Mr. Clark's office"? The latter is clearly preferable.

If he's saying neither one—if, in fact, he's just picking up with a surly "Yeah?"—it's best you know that now.

Leave a message for yourself, of relative complexity, and see if you get it—and if you get it right.

If you answer your own phone at the office, say your full name whenever you do. If the caller is taking way too long to get to the point, plead a meeting and say good-bye. Courtesy is one thing; sabotaging your own work, by losing precious time, is another.

If you have a speakerphone, use it only when absolutely necessary. Your voice is never very clear, and most callers will feel uncomfortable knowing their words are being broadcast that way. Aren't you?

If friends or family call you often at the office, discourage them from doing so. But if you enjoy calling them on your office phone, first be sure that your company is either unable to keep track of such calls, or that its policy is not to bother. A friend of mine made a practice of calling her dear old mother—in another state—almost every day. For months, there was no problem. Then, all of a sudden, there was. She was presented with a $750 phone bill, and she was able to keep her job only after abasing herself before her boss, the entire accounting department, and the head of personnel.

Write your mother a letter.

Addendum: Many Happy Returns

Another friend of mine, a Midwestern book publisher, remembers getting from his own first boss a piece of advice that has stood him in good stead ever since. "Never go home for the day until you've answered every phone call you got that day."

Can this be for real? Even the people you know you don't want to talk to? Even the ones you'd prefer to avoid forever?

Especially those.

If you don't, they'll just call back tomorrow. And the day after. And the day after that. Better to deal with it now— even if it's unpleasant—and get it over with. The other party won't take bad news any more happily just because it's been postponed. "I can't say it's been the secret of my success," my publisher friend confides, "but I can say that it's helped to give me a certain reputation for decisiveness and efficiency. People know they'll get an answer from me—even if it isn't the one they wanted to hear."

What about the people who call back anyway, hoping to inspire a change of mind?

"There is a limit. And my assistant, who answers my phone, knows when to cut things short."

Command Central

At work, you wear your office the same way you wear your suit—it surrounds you, proclaims you, displays you to the world. If your office is going to talk about you, you must be sure you know what it's saying.

• The larger your office is, the better. A corner is always good; so is a big window. Try to frame yourself in the power position—in a high-backed chair, city skyline behind you. (If your view is lousy, draw the blinds.)

• The same for your desk—the bigger, the better. But standard-issue metal desks carry no clout—go for old-fashioned burnished wood, or glass, or something high-tech.

• If, however, you happen to be a small man, scale these things down. It does nothing for your power profile to have your face peeking out from behind the stapler and your feet dangling above the floor.

• Desk sets, matching blotters, things like that, are all signs of trying too hard. Keep the surface of your desk clean and efficient—ready for action, like the bridge of a battleship.

• If you need file cabinets, try to keep them outside—in the secretary's area, for instance.

• For your visitors, provide a chair or two directly *across* the desk from you. Do not bring these chairs close in to the side of your own desk; this encroaches on your territory and undermines your authority.

• Be sure that your visitors' chairs are not higher than your own. Ideally, you should be looking down; they should be gazing up . . . at your eminence.

• If your floor is neither a good parquet nor attractively carpeted, throw down a nice rug—Persian, perhaps—to dress it up. If it's linoleum, cover every square inch.

• Don't festoon the walls with a collage of family photos, college diplomas, posters (*please*), etc. One or two things hanging on the wall is more than sufficient; it's an office, not an art gallery. (Doctors, however, may hang up all the diplomas they wish; patients find it comforting.)

• Depending on your business, you may have on the wall a chart, graph, or map. One acquaintance of mine kept a map of the world, with colored pushpins stuck in it, as if they represented something to do with his work. Very impressive. Totally bogus.

The Office Party

What merriment. What frivolity. What hilarity.

What a powder keg.

The office party has the potential to sink your career faster than a U-boat. Watch your sonar screen at all times; when any of the following five things appears on it—shoals on which your frail craft can founder in the blink of an eye—hold fast to the wheel.

(1) The bar. Unless you're sticking to Perrier (by far the wisest course), have only one drink. Nurse it. Refresh it with ice. Sip it through one of those teensy little straws. But don't order another; loose lips sink ships—your own.

(2) The boss. Just because it's a party, don't assume everybody's equal all of a sudden. Your boss won't.

(3) Your office rival. Just because it's a party, don't assume everybody's your friend. If he tried to show you up at the meeting this morning, he'll be just as anxious to make you look bad here. Give him no such opportunity.

(4) That cute first-year associate with whom you've been trading glances in the hall all month. Office romances are always risky, but they're doubly so when you launch them with everybody looking. Even if you and the new associate decide to leave together, let her go first—then meet her down in the lobby.

(5) The cleaning crew. If you're still there when they are, you stayed too long.

Love Among the Files

You know it's a bad idea. You've read all the articles. You've seen all the talk shows. But if you don't date somebody you work with, who are you going to date? You've been working till nine o'clock all week, and even if you had the strength to go out and hit the bars, nobody else could understand the kind of pressure you've been under.

But Daisy can.

Daisy's been there, right beside you. Even as you sweated out another deadline, her perfume hung in the air around you. Even as you madly crunched the numbers one more time, Daisy's sweet face kept popping in the door, "just to see how you're holding up." Even as you wondered how you'd ever get it all done, Daisy assured you, with a knowing smile, that "you always pull it off. That's why they call on you in the first place."

Daisy, god bless her . . . the most glorious creature on the thirty-third floor. And now, this radiant beauty has consented to see you, outside the office, in the real (as best you can recall it) world. Are you dreaming, you wonder?

Hold your horses.

Time for a brief reality check. Ask yourself these questions:

Am I in any way Daisy's superior in the office hierarchy?

In other words, can you affect her work status, her promotions, her salary? If so, back off. There is great potential for professional mayhem, emotional abuse, and—yes—legal action if things don't work out.

Is Daisy in any way my superior in the office hierarchy?

In other words . . . see above.

Do I really want my work life and personal life to be so commingled?

At the moment, you do—you're listening to the roar of your hormones. But in the long run, do you want to be involved with someone you see at work every day, whose career may in many ways mirror your own, who shares the same cast of characters as you do from nine to five?

Are there any advantages to such a liaison?

Sure. You both have, presumably, an interest in the same field. You both know the same people, you have tons to talk about, you can make your vacations mesh, you can share a cab to the office now and then.

Are there disadvantages?

All of the above: neither one of you brings much that's new to the relationship. Instead of a lawyer and a doctor trading news of the courtroom and the operating theater, you're both going over the same material—why the client didn't go for that new ad slogan, who they think is gonna come up with something better, why they didn't understand the marketing survey, etc. Talk about taking work home from the office—together, you're taking the office itself.

Any dangers down the road?

One biggie—and it's perfectly obvious.
If you break up, and badly, who gets custody of the job?

Even if you're on different floors, and in different departments, things can get sticky. And sometimes the only way to get them unstuck is for one of you to find a new place of employment. Could it wind up being you?

Love Among the Files: Part II

If you *are* romantically involved with somebody at the office, it's best to behave as if you weren't. For instance . . .

Do Not:

—stroll down the corridor, hand in hand, gazing into each other's eyes. One, you might crash into the mail cart; two, you will make everyone else, from the lonely to the unhappily married, want to gag.

—share knowing smiles across a meeting table. Everyone else is trying to concentrate on the annual report. It's boring enough to begin with, and if they also have to start wondering about what you two did last night—and what on earth in the annual report could be making you think of it now—it could fast become impossible.

—eat lunch together every day. Lunch is an important opportunity to bond with your fellow workers, swap information (in the form of gossip), find out what's really going on. If you're forever at a table for two, you're missing out on a lot of essential news.

—make out in the photocopying room. I know, I know, it seems so zany and wild—to you—but to everybody else it just makes photocopying even more of a hassle. First, they have to remember to whistle or cough as they approach the machines, then they have to share in the embarrassed merriment as you gather up the "witty" photocopies you just made of each other's body parts. (And are you absolutely *sure* that that light won't do you any damage?)

—send each other intimate E-mail. *Somebody* in your office knows how to crack the system—trust me—and nothing would make more popular reading than what you and your honey have been promising to do to each other with a jar of apricot jam, a goose feather, and a shoehorn later that night.

Salesmanship!

It's a word that, face it, has some negative connotations. It can summon up visions of used car dealers in loud jackets, turning back odometers. Or Willie Loman trudging the streets with his sample cases. Or motivational seminars led by guys who've never sold anything but tapes on how to sell things.

But let's face another fact—most careers are about sales, one way or the other. Move the product, improve the bottom line, get the order. A lawyer has to sell himself to his client—and later to the jury. A doctor has to sell himself to his patients, or else go into research. A teacher has to sell himself to his students, or they won't hear a word he has to say.

So taking some cues from the hard-core hucksters may not be such a bad idea. Here, some of the inside dope on selling:

• Make that first impression a great one. Show you're alert, vibrant, upbeat. Nobody likes a moper. And energy can actually be contagious.

• Attune yourself to the other person. Pay close attention to what he's saying. Don't interrupt, and don't contra-
dict. Even if you don't agree, start out by saying you see his
point. Then explain why your idea, your firm, or your service
would be the better choice. Refrain from name-calling.

• Never ask for a "no." In other words, don't say, "You
wouldn't be in need of a new computer system, would you?"
This just begs for a negative reply.

• Get the other person to say "yes" as many times as
you can. The old pros use this sales trick all the time. On the
theory that saying yes is habit-forming, they lead their pros-
pect down the path by asking him loads of questions that
bring an automatic yes. "Wouldn't you like to be driving the
most stylish automobile on the road?" Yes. "Wouldn't you
like to know that it's also the safest automobile on the road?"
Yes. "Wouldn't you want your wife and kids to enjoy such a
fabulous automobile?" Yes. And so on.

• Don't do anything sudden, disruptive, or confusing.
If you're all over the place, the guy across the table will start to
get nervous, too. Even if you're not in control, act as if you
are. Never ever point at him with a pen, pencil, Magic
Marker, ruler, swizzle stick, or loaded weapon.

• Ask for the order. In my own first job, writing ad copy
for *Esquire* Magazine, I actually wrote subscription ads in
which I never asked anyone to subscribe; I thought it would
seem pushy. On one ad, I even forgot to include the order
form; Irv, my boss (who'd paid $10,000 to place that ad),
thought it might be a good idea if we asked people to subscribe from now on and provided them with an order blank.
"Ask and ye shall receive," he told me. "Don't ask and you're
fired." From that day forward, I asked.

Your Appointed Rounds

You've got an important appointment at a customer's, or client's, office. You've got to clinch the deal, get the order, finalize the contract. To accomplish your mission, you must also remember a few simple things:

• Get there on time—but not too early. Arrive no more than ten minutes before your appointed time (even if it means cooling your heels at the newsstand downstairs). You don't want the client to think you've got nothing better to do than sit in his waiting area.

• When you're ushered into your client's office, shake hands, sit down, and socialize—briefly. Take your cues from the client, but if things look like they're never going to get around to business, bring them around yourself. You don't want to use up all your time on trivialities.

• Make your points clearly, concisely, and convincingly. To this end, you should have prepared your presentation beforehand. Try to have anticipated the client's problems, objections, or uncertainties—and have your solutions ready.

• If this meeting is definitely going to require a follow-up, have some materials to leave behind—a précis of the proposal, an outline of the deal, a sketch. Assuming that the client is going to have to ponder some of this material or information before coming to his own decision, you want to have made that as easy as possible for him to do.

• Don't linger. When the necessary business has been concluded, or you've done all you can do, don't wait for the client to find a graceful way to get you out of his office. Thank him for his time, stand up, close your briefcase, and be on your way.

• That same day, send a note to thank him again for meeting with you, and to say that you'll be calling the next week to see if a decision has been made. The idea is to stay (courteously) on top of things, and to keep your business transaction at the fore.

• Do call back when you said you would.

Impressing the Boss

This is at once one of the most crucial and one of the trickiest assignments you will ever undertake in the business world. Your associates will be trying to outgun you at every turn, your boss will be skeptical and wary, and as a result your efforts will have to be as subtle as they are ingenious.

And yet, you must persevere.

The first thing to deal with is your normal human reluctance to shamelessly promote your own self-interest. Your mother may have told you not to be a braggart, your father may have reminded you that "talent will out," your Zen instructor may have counseled you that "all things come to him who does not seek them."

The only thing that comes to him who does not seek it is jury duty. If it's career advancement you're after, you will have to impress the boss.

How? By following some fundamental strategies:

• Log in the hours. There is nothing more deadly to a career than getting to work at 10 o'clock sharp, only to find that your boss has left three messages for you to come to his office—whenever you get in. Equally deadly, however, is to be seen breezing past his office at five o'clock, and waving good-night while he pores over the latest company reports.

Even if it means bringing a paperback thriller to work, and reading it quietly behind your closed door, make sure that you're present and accounted for.

· Keep a tidy, organized office. You never know when your superior may pop in for a quick consultation, and you don't want to have to brush a Burger King bag off the guest chair before he can sit down. Nor do you want him to have to talk to you across a desk cluttered with college baseball trophies and framed photos of your fiancée on the beach at Cape May. The personal memorabilia should be kept to a very discreet minimum.

· Take your dress cues from the guy you work for. Sure, he's older, richer, higher up the corporate ladder. But if he's natty and well groomed, chances are he appreciates the same in those around him. If he wears an open collar and chinos, then he may be put off if you show up in a pin-striped suit every day. (For one TV job, I had to come back after the initial interview, because the producer—a *very* casual sort—thought I looked like a Philadelphia banker. Only after I showed up in an approximation of his work clothes—a sweater and jeans—did he feel it was possible that I could indeed be "creative.")

· Volunteer. Volunteer, first, for the extra duties around the office—not emptying the wastebaskets, of course, but compiling the stats, or planning the corporate retreat. Anything which will bring you further notice, and ideally, contact with the senior partners in the firm.

And, if you're feeling particularly clever, volunteer for a cause or charity outside the firm—one that you happen to know the higher-ups are already involved with. When you bump into them at an event sponsored by that charity (and contributing cash is always a quick way to make your way in), remember to feign surprise. Give the impression that your concern for this cause is a long-standing one: "When I was a boy, one of my closest friends was a blue-legged tree frog, and ever since that time I've been devoted to creating a national swampland for their preservation."

· If your boss happens to be a woman, an increasingly common situation these days, do NOT treat her that way. Do not compliment her on her dress each morning, do not try to pull out her chair at meetings, do not give her flowers on the closing of that big deal. She will see this as sexist, demeaning, or at the very least discomfiting—and she will be dead right. You may be the most dashing cavalier on your own time, but at the office you are her employee—and subordinate.

Business Gifts

Oh, sure, there are plenty of unkind words for gifts you give your business contacts—words such as bribe, kickback, graft—but we both know you're not guilty of that. (One way to tell? Ask yourself if you'd have felt more comfortable bestowing this particular gift in a brown paper sack in the back booth of Nunzio's; if you would have, you're probably skating on thin ice.)

There are many perfectly legitimate occasions for giving business gifts—Christmas, for instance, or to thank someone for having done you a great favor (such as introducing you to the Saudi Minister of Finance). And on those occasions, it's important to address some important questions, most notably:

Who pays? Many companies, including the one you work for, may have a standard item they mass-produce and that you are encouraged to send to your customers or clients. Often, it will bear some kind of company logo or identification. Send one of these, and it's obviously at company expense.

But there are times when you may want to send something else, something better, something more distinctive. Some companies will provide you with automatic reimbursement; others will want you to get an okay in advance. On occasion, you'll decide simply to go for it—to buy the gift at your own expense. (The government will help out, with a small tax deduction per gift.) Whatever, you shouldn't go overboard—any normal business gift should not exceed, say, $150 in value; beyond that, and you might as well be back at Nunzio's.

What's the usual range? If you're a junior exec, you might want to stay in the $40 to $50 area. If you're a little farther along in your career, you might wish to lay out another sawbuck on each of your gifts. If you're senior level? Maybe a hundred. David Geffen? There's no telling.

If you have a secretary or assistant, you should give him or her something nice but innocuous—a Christmas plant, a $25 gift certificate, a handsome hardcover book. Jewelry is not a good idea, nor are items of apparel (all are too easily misconstrued). If, however, this person has worked faithfully by your side for several years, the gift should be commensurately greater.

Secretaries often give presents in return (though they are under no obligation to do so); their present to you should be appropriately modest (a tin of homemade brownies, for instance).

What do you give? At holiday times, there are a zillion catalogues offering gourmet food baskets, which are easy to send and hard to offend anyone with. Even if they hate the smoked sausage, they'll like the cheese.

At other times, you may send anything from a set of compact discs to a stylish fountain pen. But with two of the more popular items—flowers and alcohol—there are several things to think about first.

Flowers may now be sent by men and women to men and women alike: that's the standard wisdom (though I still shudder when someone sends flowers to me). But if you've been invited to the senior partner's house for dinner, do not arrive with a bouquet in hand; hosts do not want to have to go looking for a vase.

Flowers sent the next day, in thanks, should be cut (if going to a home) or in an arrangement (if going to an office).

But do be sure, before sending flowers to a residence, that your recipient is still in town. Nothing like arriving back home to find a bunch of wilted flowers on the doorstep.

Alcohol is tricky, too. Are you quite confident that the person is not a teetotaler? You should be. Assuming your recipient does drink, do you know what, exactly? Not much point in sending Scotch to a vodka drinker. That's one reason wine is a good idea: it's always useful.

But if you bring a bottle with you to a dinner party, do not expect the host to open and serve it on the spot; chances are, he's picked out his own wine, and it's already "breathing" in the kitchen or pantry. Expect him to put yours away for another time.

By and large, it's wiser not to send wine or spirits to a person's office; his or her home is more appropriate.

Asking for It

Sometimes it comes up in the form of a semiannual review. Sometimes it's done at a meeting requested expressly for this purpose. But if you're in business, you will have to ask—many times in the course of your career—for a raise.

Believe it or not, many people feel they don't really deserve a raise, even though they'd like one. If you're one of these people, stop thinking that way. As Jack Benny once said when accepting an award, "I don't deserve this . . . but then, I've got arthritis, and I don't deserve that, either." Business is a game, and your salary in large measure indicates how well you're playing. (And think about it, some night while you're burning the midnight oil and your boss is on a ski trip to Aspen—is *he* really worth what *he's* paid?) Before heading into any salary negotiation, conquer your own inner demons. Or at least shut them up.

And while you're at it, keep quiet yourself. The first mistake many people make is to start babbling before they even hit the chair—spilling out what they need, why they need it, how bad they feel about asking for it, other offers they've recently turned down, what being a part of this company means to them. Stifle it. Let your superior dictate the tone and pace of the meeting—at least at the start.

Never forget this is a business negotiation—not a therapy session or personality evaluation. Keep your emotions out of it. Sure, they play a part—Why else were you tossing and turning in bed all night?—but don't let your emotions take hold of you now. A cool head stands a much better chance of prevailing.

By the same token, emotional appeals—heart-wrenching stories of fiscal woe, medical problems, family obligations—just make you look incapable of managing your life. Even if the tales are true, listening to them tends to embarrass the guy sitting on the other side of the desk. And this embarrassment doesn't make him want to give you what you want—it makes him want to get you out of his office before your tears leave a spot on the carpet.

What *should* you do? You should prepare yourself with facts, arguments, and information that will bolster your case and neutralize his. If he says he'd like to give you a raise, but the company has had a really bad year, know in advance if that's true. How bad? And how bad in comparison to other companies in the same industry? If he says nobody's getting a raise this year, try to have in your arsenal the reliable information that somebody else already has gotten one—and how much. (You don't have to cite the specifics—you can just say you know that other people in the department have.)

Be prepared, too, to cite your own contributions in the past year. If you brought in a new client, say so. If you took over the duties of someone who left without being replaced, say so. If you've been putting in immense amounts of unpaid overtime, say so—and here, provide some figures to back it up. (Using an office diary, note any overtime you're putting in, and before your salary negotiation, add it up. You'll probably be surprised at what it comes to, and so will he.)

On the question of naming your figure, there is much disagreement. Some experts say, declare exactly how much you want; others say, see what happens. I suggest a middle course: know exactly what your figure is, and if you don't hear a specific offer forthcoming, then ask for that figure. Be sure, however, that that figure is at least ten or twenty percent higher than what you're actually willing, in the last analysis, to accept. You want the other guy to feel that he saved the company *some* money.

Are there also some other things you might like—a larger expense account, membership in a business club downtown, more vacation time, a secretary you don't have to share? Now is the time to bring these things up, too—and in the general negotiation, you can always sacrifice some straight salary for concessions on these other matters.

Finally, try to get a firm answer. Yes or no, and how much exactly. If the person you're talking to really has to refer the matter elsewhere, get a firm date by which you can expect to hear. And don't be shy—if you don't hear by that time, follow up immediately. If you don't, and you let things just sort of drag along, you'll have undone all the trouble you took to appear energetic and in charge.

Yiddish 101

You don't have to be Jewish to act *meshugah*. To suspect that the boss is a *gonif*. Or to behave like a *mensch*.

You just have to know what the words mean. Yiddish, a mixture of German and Hebrew with some Slavic thrown in, is as American as pastrami on rye, and it has become a critical component of the national business vocabulary (particularly in show biz). As such, it's important that you understand, and on occasion be able to utilize, some of the basic terms. What follows are key words, each defined and used in a sample sentence.

meshugah: crazy. "The guy's *meshugah*; he put that no-good brother-in-law of his on the payroll."

gonif: thief, crook. "I knew he was a *gonif* the minute I saw him eyeing the till."

chutzpah: nerve, moxie. "Talk about *chutzpah*—he walked onto the studio lot without an appointment and demanded to see the head of production."

schnorrer: someone who manages to wheedle, or con, or "borrow" whatever he wants. Free of charge, of course. "Such a *schnorrer*—every time he saw the check coming, he excused himself to go to the bathroom."

schmooze: to mingle socially, often with an ulterior motive. "He'd hang around the bar at the Bel-Air Hotel, *schmoozing* with anybody in the business."

kibbitzing: chitchat. Trading news, gossip, stories. "Hi, I just called to *kibbitz*—what happened at that party last night? Was you-know-who there?"

shmendrick: a fool, someone who doesn't count for much (also known as a *shmiggege*). "What a *shmendrick*—you could sell him the Brooklyn Bridge, and he'd thank you for it."

schlemiel: another word for someone who's inept, or clumsy. A *schlemiel* spills his soup—

and the person he spills it on is known as a *schli-mazl.*

"Oy, vay is meer": literally, "Oh, woe is me!" An all-purpose expression, it's sometimes used after good, as well as bad, experiences. But always accompanied by a sigh or groan.

mensch: a good and decent person. "He's a real *mensch*—even though she cleaned him out in the divorce, he still sends her a birthday card every year."

As far as the pronunciation of these words goes, I could try to give it to you phonetically, but if you haven't ever heard them used, the best thing to do is to go into a Jewish deli and ask the guy behind the counter to say them out loud for you.

And buy a knish to thank him.

"I'm *What?*"

Fired. It can happen to anyone, at any time. And not necessarily through any fault of your own. The company's being downsized. A key client was lost. The chairman wants to hire his best friend, for your position.

What do you do?

Get a grip. Then deal with the consequences.

First of all, do make sure that they understand, and you understand, that you are being fired. Don't offer your resignation. If you're fired, you're entitled to lots of things, most notably unemployment insurance, that you won't be entitled to if it looks like you left by choice.

Insist on the vacation pay you've accumulated, which usually poses no problem, and then ask what kind of severance package they're offering, which usually does.

Customarily an employer will offer, when pressed, one week of severance pay for each year you've worked there. Try to get two.

Then work on protecting your vested interests—is there a pension or profit-sharing plan in which you've been participating? Make sure you protect your rights, and what you've already invested.

And what about your health plan? Get the company to extend your coverage for as long as possible, and find out what it will cost you to convert it to an individual policy later. Then shop around to see if you can find a better policy elsewhere.

If you can stand to hang around the place, ask to use an empty office, a free desk, phone line, etc., from which to conduct your search for new employment. (Personally, when I was fired it was in the late morning, and I was in such a hurry to get out of there I asked if it would be all right if I didn't come back from lunch. I was told that that would be fine.)

Even if you, too, would rather get out quick (or if you've been given no choice), don't skulk out the door before anyone so much as knows what's happened to you. Tell anyone and everyone who might be sympathetic, and especially tell anyone and everyone who might know of some leads. "There but for the grace of God" will be going through all of their heads, and now, more than ever, they'll be ready to help. In a couple of weeks, they'll have forgotten what you looked like.

Finally, if you can swallow your indignation long enough, write a cordial note to the head of the company, with a copy to the personnel department, thanking them for the opportunities they've provided in the past, and for the things you were able to accomplish in your time there (detailing a few of these accomplishments, too, if you like). After all, these are the people whom potential employers will probably be contacting, to find out more about you. And what you want those new prospects to find out is that you're this incredibly well-mannered and unflappable guy.

Which, of course, you are.

CHAPTER V

In Polite Society

———◦———

"He was a bold man that first eat an oyster."

—JONATHAN SWIFT,
Polite Conversation (c. 1738)

The Art of Conversation

You'll notice it's always called the "art" of conversation, never the science. There are no hard and fast rules here— it's a fluid situation, one that calls for you always to be on your toes and attentive to every subtle change in the wind. Are you still explaining your Oswald conspiracy theory while everyone else has moved on to dog grooming? Have you noticed that the more you speak, the fewer people there are left in the room? Are you wondering why there were no follow-up questions to the graphic account of your splenec-tomy?

Even in the absence of hard data, there are some general

conversational guidelines that may help you to win friends and influence people. And there are more than a few things you would do well to avoid.

Do Not:

—answer the question, "How are you?" with a factual reply. No one's really asking. If you're so unwell you feel it has to be mentioned, you shouldn't be out at all—go home and get in bed.

—begin every sentence with "I." Fascinating as you are, other people may eventually feel swamped by the relentless tide of self-promotion, and set sail.

—tell jokes. Now many people consider this an ice breaker, and a wonderful conversational gambit ... but they're wrong. Jokes are politically dangerous (somebody's got to be the butt of each one), they require excellent—and uninterrupted—timing (which you won't get), and they can stop genuine conversation faster than a blaring stereo.

—monopolize the air time. Artful conversation is an exchange of ideas and views. If you end a conversation with someone whose name you didn't catch, whose thoughts you still don't know, and whose voice you would never recognize, chances are you were just a tad overbearing.

—discuss anything requiring an actual dollar sign. Not how much you make, not how much your house cost, not how much you're wondering your host's house cost, not what your wife spends on clothes, not what you're paying to join the country club, not what your stamp collection is worth, not what you lost in Las Vegas, not what you're counting on your great Aunt Agatha to leave you . . . you get the picture. Money's verboten.

—talk about business in a social setting. Even if you meet the connection of your dreams, now is not the time to try to make your pitch. Do your best to charm him and make a favorable impression, and if you would like to pursue a business angle, discreetly hand him your card and say you'll call his office to make an appointment.

Do:

—remember to include the people seated on both sides of you at a dinner party. It is a traditional rule, though one seldom observed anymore, to begin the meal by speaking to the person on your right, and then, with the arrival of the next course, to turn and engage the person on your left. And so on, with each course.

—maintain good eye contact. Focus on the person who's talking to you, and even if Heather Locklear walks in, glances over at you, licks her lips, and beckons, wait until the person talking to you has finished—or reached a natural pause—before excusing yourself to vault across the table.

—sustain a body posture that expresses that you are both interested and alert. Sitting up straight, leaning forward slightly, and cocking your head are all signs that you are paying attention; slouching in your chair, leaning back, and yawning are pretty clear indications you are not.

—overlook mistakes in the other person's grammar, pronunciation, and (in most cases) facts. This isn't a formal debate, you won't get any points for winning, and if you start issuing correctives, the other person, rightfully embarrassed, will silently swear revenge on you and all your descendants.

—ask questions of the other person, and listen to their replies. You will be considered a brilliant conversationalist if you do nothing more than skillfully draw out other people. In retrospect, all they'll remember is how enthralling the conversation (all about themselves) was.

Let Us Now Praise

If you're ever in doubt about whether to compliment someone on something, doubt no more—do it. Nothing is as inexpensive to offer, and as happily received, as praise. It's the grease that keeps life from sticking to the griddle, and you can never spread enough of it around.

When offering praise, you must do it unsolicited. If the other person had to ask for it, it doesn't count. What you want to do is surprise the recipient with the good news: "You've done a great job on that presentation!" "I've never been to a better party." "You have the best taste of anyone I know."

Do not append to your praise anything conditional— "You've done a great job on that presentation, given the time constraints, budget limitations, and obvious problems with the material itself." This is not praise—this is a veiled critique.

Nor should praise trail after it a favor: "You have the best taste of anyone I know—would you mind redecorating my apartment for me?" Even if you have a secret agenda, keep it secret for the time being.

Accepting praise is, in some ways, harder than giving it. Most of us don't know how to take a compliment. Confronted with one, we either sheepishly demur, or flat-out deny it: "Me? Good taste? I'm color blind, as any fool can see, and I failed every art class I ever took." Well, that was suave—now you've not only lowered your own stock, you've also managed to make the other person look like a nincompoop for complimenting you.

When complimented, look your fan straight in the eye, say "Thank you so much—I appreciate that," and graciously turn the conversation to another topic. Now you'll look modest and unassuming, to boot.

Speechifying

In surveys to determine what people fear the most, public speaking has always been at or near the top of the list. In some cases, it's ranked ahead of dying.

And yet, all of us will be called, at one time or another, to speak in front of a group. It may just be offering the best man's toast at a wedding, or running a focus group at the office. Or it could be addressing a huge, hostile shareholders' meeting, as chairman of the board.

Whatever, some rules of speechifying always hold.

· When deciding what you want to say, figure out how you'd *say it*—not how you'd write it. The two forms of communication are very different. Spoken language is less formal, more direct; if you can't manage to say something easily, and without catching a breath, find a different way of putting it.

• If you're pretty glib, just use note cards, or a brief outline of what you want to say. This will allow you to sound spontaneous and at ease. If you're not so gifted, type out your speech, all in capital letters, triple-spaced, with breaks between paragraphs and clearly numbered pages. Rehearse it enough so that you feel comfortable, but not so much that you wind up sounding canned.

• Tell a joke or two, *if you're good at it.* People love to laugh, and it gets them on your side.

If you're not good at telling jokes, this is not the time to try. Flop sweat can ruin a new suit in a matter of seconds.

• Remember that if you're speaking from up on a stage, or in front of a large group, your gestures must be a little broader, your intonation a little more forceful. The minute people hear a mike, they expect to be entertained, and while they may not expect you to be Elvis, they do want to be caught up in your speech or presentation.

• Also, if the assembly is a large one, and you're speaking from some distance, don't wear anything that's either so flashy it will distract people from your message, or so subtle that you'll be washed out. Small checks, pinstripes, and such are not as wise an idea as a solid dark suit and white shirt. You want to present a clear, forceful profile.

• Don't open yourself to questions or other interruptions unless you really feel you can keep control of your audience, and stay on track. Otherwise, one little digression can leave you stranded and completely lost.

· If you're nervous, disregard utterly that old bit of wisdom that says you should look out at the crowd and imagine them all in their underwear. Could there be anything *more* unsettling? No, if you're nervous, just remember to take slow, deep breaths, and if you must, rely on your typescript for the first minute or two. Have an ally well positioned so that when you do look up, you have a friendly face to gaze upon.

Do not take a tranquilizer—its effect could be greater than you planned. (My brother did that just before his wedding, and the poor guy still thinks he's single.)

Put It There

If this weren't done so badly, so often, there'd be no need to say these things. But when shaking hands, it's important that you expend a little effort.

Shake firmly, but not brutally. And offer your whole hand, not three fingers.

If you know your hand is damp, give it a quick wipe on your pants leg, or fan it in the air. If your hand is as cold as a Popsicle, and you can discreetly manage to do so, warm it up by sitting on it for a second, or wedging it into your armpit.

And finally, a couple of seconds after you have clasped the other person's hand, let go. Shaking hands is not a license to take someone prisoner.

Language Lab

"What can I say—she has that *je ne sais quoi* [indescribable something] that drives men wild."

"Love is the *lingua franca* [common language] of the world."

"It's a dinner for Prince Charles—black tie is *de rigueur* [absolutely required]."

They call it English, but in fact our spoken tongue is peppered with foreign and antique expressions that often crop up in our daily affairs. To spice up your own conversation—and to be sure that you understand what other people might be getting at—here are some of the more common and useful foreign words and phrases you might bump into.

Latin

quid pro quo: one thing in return for another. "I'll give you the stock options if you'll drop the lawsuit—we'll make it an even *quid pro quo*."

carpe diem: seize the day. "You'll never get a better chance to pop the question to her—*carpe diem*."

Sic transit gloria mundi: So passes the glory of this world.

Nota bene: Note this well.

De gustibus non est disputandum: There's no accounting for taste.

Et tu, Brute?: And you, too, Brutus? (What Caesar said to his friendly assassin, Brutus, on the steps of the Senate. What you, too, might say to a friend who has turned on you.)

rara avis: rare bird; a wonderful thing.

hoi polloi: the commoners; rifraff.

vox populi: the voice of the people; popular opinion.

tabula rasa: a clean slate.

Veni, vidi, vici: I came, I saw, I conquered. (Caesar said it first.)

Vita brevis, ars longa: Life is short, art endures.

ex cathedra: from the chair; carrying great authority, as if from the Pope.

ne plus ultra: the acme; highest point.

prima facie: on the face of it; at first glance.

e pluribus unum: from many, one. (If this sounds familiar, it's because it's the motto of the United States.)

deus ex machina: an outside force that unexpectedly enters and resolves a crisis (usually used in the context of a play or movie). "If it weren't for the *deus ex machina*—when her long-lost brother reappears with the ray-gun—they'd never have escaped from the alien spaceship."

In vino veritas: In wine, there is truth.

sub rosa: in strict confidence; secret.

ars gratia artis: art for art's sake.

mens sana in corpore sano: a sound mind in a sound body.

French

Plus ça change, plus c'est la même chose: The more things change, the more they stay the same.

Où sont les neiges d'antan?: Where are the snows of yesteryear?

épater le bourgeois: to shock the middle class. (The goal of avant-garde artists, who regard everyone else as Philistines.)

succès d'estime: an artistic and critical success (but one which the public probably didn't go for).

fait accompli: something that's already over and done.

faux pas: a false step; a blunder in etiquette.

idée fixe: fixed idea; a rooted preconception.

ancien régime: old regime. ("When the new boss took over, she fired everybody in that department except for Sam—he's the only survivor of the *ancien régime*.")

chacun à son goût: each to his own taste.

droit du seigneur: the Lord's Right (traditionally, to enjoy the bride before her vassal husband did on the wedding night).

noblesse oblige: privilege carries with it responsibilities.

Cherchez la femme!: Look for the woman. (This saying presumes that a woman, or the love of one, serves as the cause or instigation of most things that go on in life. It could be right.)

entre nous: between you and me. ("*Entre nous*, I think Wilfrid is cheating on his wife again.")

comme ci, comme ça: so-so; middling.

comme il faut: as it should be done; proper.

Italian

dolce far niente: the sweetness of doing nothing; happy idleness.

La donna è mobile: The woman is fickle. (Listen to Act IV of Verdi's *Rigoletto* for more.)

giusto: exact; in the correct measure.

cognoscenti: the experts; those who particularly understand and appreciate something.

al fresco: in the fresh air. "It's such a lovely terrace—why don't we dine right here, *al fresco?*"

prima donna: an opera star (and usually one who's hard to handle).

a cappella: in the church style, meaning without instrumental accompaniment. ("I just love *a cappella* music—barbershop quartets are my favorite.")

Spanish

Mi casa es su casa: My house is your house. (Make yourself at home.)

mañana: morning; tomorrow. "I'm too pooped—we can always do it *mañana.*"

de nada: not at all; you're welcome.

De noche, todos los gatos son pardos: At night all cats are gray.

aficionado: an avid fan. "He's a real *aficionado*—he's had season tickets for the past twenty years."

con mucho gusto: with pleasure; gladly.

German

Gemütlichkeit: an air of warm congeniality; cozy.

Sturm und Drang: storm and stress; turmoil.

Nicht wahr?: Isn't it true?

Hausfrau: housewife. (Today, use this one, if at all, advisedly.)

Angst: anxiety, dread. ("I don't know what's wrong with me—I guess it's just an attack of *Angst*—but I can't seem to calm down and concentrate.")

Weltanschauung: world-view; personal perspective on life. ("The whole idea of equality between the sexes—it just doesn't jibe with his *Weltanschauung*.")

Weltschmerz: a melancholy, world-weary state of mind.

Zeitgeist: the prevailing intellectual spirit of a time.

Schadenfreude: mean-spirited joy and relief (usually at someone else's misfortune).

"May I Introduce?"

So many once valuable arts have been lost to us over the ages. Nobody can fresco a ceiling like Michelangelo anymore, nobody can mummify a pharaoh like the ancient Egyptians, and nobody, but nobody, knows how to perform an introduction anymore.

Think of all the times you've entered a social or business gathering, only to find yourself helplessly marooned, introduced to no one, left to fend for yourself. Or the times you *have* been introduced, but so badly that you never had a chance to catch the other person's name, to correct the pronunciation of your own, or to figure out who this new person is.

Even for something as seemingly simple and natural as an introduction, there are some age-old rules to observe: for one thing, if you're the host of the gathering, be sure that you greet all your guests when they arrive and make sure, if they don't already know everyone, that they are introduced to someone else they might like to meet.

As for the actual introduction, say each person's name clearly, so that neither one has to ask again later, and consider adding a few complimentary words about each one's accomplishments. People like to meet other important or praiseworthy people. The first person I observed to practice this on a regular basis was the brilliant and engaging Bert Greene, the writer and world-class cook, whose parties were always joyous occasions. Taking you by the elbow, Bert would say something like, "Robert Masello, I'd like you to meet Alice Jones, who puts together those fabulous shows at the Matrix Gallery. Robert has just written the book that definitively refutes quantum mechanics." Then, even if he had to leave the two of us together to go answer the door, we had somewhere to start. And each of us thought we were already in the swim.

Younger people are usually introduced *to* older people: In other words, your girlfriend is introduced *to* your grandfather. "Don Giovanni, I'd like to introduce you to Guadalupe, the woman I hope to make my wife." And at more formal gatherings, a good rule of thumb to remember is that you generally introduce more junior people to more senior people: you introduce your secretary *to* Ms. Monroe, the chief of your department, not the other way around: "Ms. Monroe, I'd like to present Linda Stewart, the new associate in the marketing department." If someone has a proper title—a judge, a doctor, an unindicted Congressman—it's a good, and gracious, idea to use the title when making the introductions.

Finally, the time may come when you have to introduce yourself to somebody, solo. Even if you've met this person before, do him or her a favor and, while sticking out your hand, say your own name. "Hi there, Hillary. Robert Masello—isn't that Bill over by the buffet table?"

The Name of Love

You're crazy about her. But she's not your wife.

You share an apartment. But you're not married.

You go everywhere together. But you don't wear wedding bands.

So what do you call her? How is she introduced?

Only in the last couple of decades has this really become a problem. People used to keep their private lives private. Now we're open and aboveboard, we do as we please and no one (with the exception of certain evangelical ministers) cares. But we still don't have a proper word for our . . . see what I mean?

The choices, such as they are, include:

Significant other. Makes one wonder if there is also an "insignificant" other, and possibly other others, too.

Partner. Sounds like someone with whom you share a small business venture, such as a pet shop or accounting practice.

Girlfriend. Fine if you're both sixteen, but after that politically incorrect.

Friend. Well, yes, of course you're friends. But you're friends with Buzz and Steve, too, and you wouldn't step into a bubble bath with them.

Lover. More than most people wish to have conjured up for them.

Sweetheart. Both saccharine and juvenile. (Ditto for *honey, li'l darlin', main squeeze,* etc.)

Cohabitant. Sounds like something off a census form.

So what's the right answer? "Julie."

Just say, "I'd like you to meet Julie," sling an arm loosely around her shoulders, and the point is made. (But you do understand that if her name isn't Julie, you should substitute her own name in that sentence? Just checking.)

First Date Etiquette

Yes, things have changed since Edith Wharton roamed the earth. Women have muscles, men use moisturizers, and everyone exchanges blood tests and health certificates before giving out their private fax lines. Yessiree, it's a brave new world out there . . .

. . . but some things haven't changed.

No matter how we try to defy it, encoded in our DNA is vital information on how to behave on a first date. This knowledge is primitive and instinctual, and in some respects flies in the face of progressive sexual philosophy.

What does this first-date behavior dictate? For men, it includes the following:

• Make the call. Do we really need to hear about this again? If you haven't got the guts to make the first overture, how will you ever make it as far as smooching, or—God forbid—*unbuttoning*?

• Pick her up at her home, office, wherever—but don't suggest meeting on some street corner at six, or at the restaurant. If you care enough to ask her out, escort her wherever you've decided to take her.

• And do take her. Make the decision. For a first date, you do not want to call someone up, then wind up saying, "So I don't know—what do *you* want to do?" Have a plan.

• But don't have a plan that rivals D-Day in complexity. Make sure it allows for time spent in free and easy conversation. You don't want to go see a movie, meet twelve friends for drinks, head to a club to hear Jack Hammer and the Decibels, and then find yourself alone at home, at four in the morning, wondering who you've just gone out with.

• While you are talking, be sure to listen. Many women are adept at drawing you out; they're practiced listeners. Learn from them. If all you've heard for the past half hour is the drone of your own voice, turn it off. Ask her a question, and then hold your fire for at least as long as it takes her to answer it. You might even go for broke, and ask a follow-up question.

• Pay up. Even today, there is nothing quite so killing to romance as a man studying the check, and saying, "Okay, let's see, you had two drinks and the Caesar salad . . ."

• Escort her home. Drop her off at the bus stop, and chances are that'll be the last time you ever see her. And deservedly so.

• Remain chaste. It's a dangerous world out there these days—one in which sex with the wrong person can cost you dearly. But holding off has other advantages, too: a man who shows restraint looks sophisticated, in control, and even a bit mysterious.

• Call the next day. This proves, beyond a shadow of a doubt, that you're not just some fly-by-night operator. It helps to establish a bedrock of trust—without which you'll never get anywhere. In love, or in life.

Flirting

Once, in the heat of the Sexual Revolution, it was considered a dead art. But flirting today is back with a vengeance.

We have to take our fun where we can find it nowadays.

To get the most out of flirting, however, it's best to remember just what it is, and what it isn't.

Flirting is not merely the overture to sex. Flirting can be, and generally is, an end in itself. Think of it as an entertaining, enjoyable practice, something that makes you feel vibrant and attractive, and you're doing fine.

Think of it, however, as the unavoidable spadework you have to do before getting somebody into bed, and you will not only miss the point, you'll also wind up watching a lot of *Star Trek* reruns all by yourself.

How do you flirt properly? While women are conceded to be the experts at this, men can certainly manage a few tricks of their own. For instance:

· The fleeting glance is always effective. The idea is to catch her eye, then look away, as if her beauty has nearly blinded you.

Then glance back . . . *because you cannot help yourself.*

· Your opening line should be simple and straightforward. (Too clever, and it looks like you've been working on it for weeks.) And please, remember that any woman over twelve has already heard those lame attempts like, "So, you must be a model."

Be original.

· Touch her (if things are going well), but very discreetly. A light grazing of her elbow, a momentary pat on the back of the hand, a touch on the wrist. Stay well clear of the erogenous zones, and always above the equator. And do it casually, as if to merely punctuate a conversational point.

She'll know what's really going on.

· Move on after a while. If you're at a party, for example, don't try to monopolize her. Maintain a little mystery by excusing yourself, and then, just when she's begun to wonder what happened to that charming fellow who knew so much about the canapés, reappear.

• Be aware of changing weather patterns. If she remains warm and engaging, flirting in return, stay with it as long as you like. If, on the other hand, you begin to feel a chill, don't wait for the frost to form on your eyelashes. Tip your imaginary hat (you weren't wearing a real one, were you?) and be on your way.

Let her repent at leisure.

Love and War

In even the sunniest of romantic relationships, the occasional thunderstorm will erupt. Who, after all, can agree on absolutely everything?

But even in the midst of the most heated argument, some rules of combat must prevail. To wit:

• No charges must be leveled, or arguments begun, in the presence of third parties. Fighting, like sex, must be done in private.

• No extraneous issues, ancient grudges, or unrelated gripes may be dragged in to further complicate the quarrel. Stick to the problem at hand.

• But do dig a bit—are you really arguing about whose turn it is to empty the dishwasher, or are you arguing about the division of the domestic responsibilities in general? Might as well settle the real issue.

• Don't get defensive. Even though we all know nobody's perfect, we all suspect that we are in fact the exception to the rule. Allow for the possibility, however remote, that you've been wrong.

　• And listen—not only to the charges being brought, but to what your partner might be leaving unsaid. Listen for what she might be having some trouble putting into words.

　• Frame your own complaint in a less confrontational way. Instead of pointing a finger and saying, "Whenever we have to go somewhere, you're never ready on time," instead try something like "I hate to be late for engagements—it makes me nervous and irritable."

　• Cool your jets. If you feel your temper rising beyond the boiling point, or if the quarrel is getting way too vindictive or personal, call a truce. Stop in time, and later on, after you've both had a chance to relax, you can always pick up where you left off.

　• Don't try to *win* the argument. It's not about winning or losing—it's about overcoming a problem, about coming up with a solution that both of you can live with.

　If all you ever want to do is win arguments, open a law office. At least you'll get paid for it.

Giving Thanks

Remember that five dollars your Uncle Leo sent you for your fifth birthday? Did you ever send him a thank-you note? Or even one of your trademark drawings of a knight in armor?

　Of course not.

　And how about that savings bond from Grandma? Did you ever do anything more than mumble into the phone after your mother dragged you over and slapped the receiver into your hand?

Guilty again.

So the last thing you probably want to hear, yet again, is to send thank-you notes, but the older you are, the more important it becomes.

These days the art of written correspondence is almost entirely lost. By sending even the simplest handwritten note, for a dinner party you've attended, a favor that was done you, a gift you've received, you will astonish and delight your addressees. They may get, and forget, a dozen phone calls that same day, but your note they'll remember.

And don't be put off by your vestigial knowledge of how to do it properly, with monogrammed stationery, fountain pen, sealing wax, family crest, etc. That's great if you can do it that way, but if you can't, don't use that as an excuse for not doing it at all. If your handwriting's hopeless, then type it. If the only letterhead you've got is on your computer screen, then use that. Be brief, polite, and sincere—and even if you did just pull the page out of your printer, do sign your name in ink.

Then drop the note in the mail forthwith—and allow at least five days for the U.S. mail to get it across the street.

Addendum: Giving Grief

On occasion you will be tempted to send notes that do not thank people, but, to be blunt, give them grief instead.

The woman who stood you up for a drink. The business associate who swiped your best account. The neighbor whose new treehouse now commands a bird's-eye view of your bedroom.

By all means, write these notes. Vent your spleen. Spill your rage onto the page. Aerate your anger.

Then, just before wasting a stamp on the envelope, drop it in the wastebasket. And go out and see a movie. The next day, you'll be glad you did.

Rule of thumb: that which is composed in anger should be disposed of in private.

If, as it happens, you still feel the weight of injustice pressing on your soul, then do go ahead and register your complaint. But compose this second missive with a cooler head and a more reasoned argument.

And even so, don't count on getting any results; it may have to be enough that you got it off your chest, and onto somebody else's.

All Apologies

"Sorry" does indeed seem to be the hardest word to say. First, it's hard to believe you could possibly have done anything wrong. (Come on already, who knew your friend's dog would have such a hard time downing a single jalapeño pepper? People eat 'em all the time.) Second, it's hard to find the right way of conveying your regrets.

But—if you are to function in polite society—you must learn the basic form of the apology.

It starts with being direct and unequivocal. Any apology that begins with a long oration on why you did what you did (the dog asked for it) or why you never showed up (the train missed the station) or what you really meant when you said she looked like she'd gained thirty pounds (you thought the weight looked *good* on her) is not an apology at all. It's a defense of yourself, and you're right back where you started—needing to issue an apology.

If finding the appropriate words is always hard for you, just keep it simple: try something like, "I'm so sorry for what happened on Saturday. I hope you'll accept my heartfelt apologies." If, for instance, it has to do with that dog, you might add, "And please send me the veterinarian's bill." Compensation for any actual damage you may have caused someone, by setting fire to their house, wearing their Tiffany lampshade on your head, or driving over their rosebushes, is highly recommended.

Depending on the seriousness of the crime, you can offer your apology in person, by mail, or over the phone (provided, of course, they'll take your call). Whichever course you choose, be prompt. An apology that is issued three weeks after the fact is considered, by virtue of the delay alone, to be grudging.

And don't burden an apology with excess baggage. Let it be. For instance, if you stood someone up at the altar, don't suggest getting married this *coming* Saturday instead. Give the other person time to accept your regrets, and even respond to them. Then, when some time has passed, you may suggest some remedy. (If not, their lawyer might.)

Great Visitations

Your friend is unwell. In fact, your friend is so unwell he's in the hospital.

What should you do?

You might pretend you never heard about it, thereby saving yourself the unhappy chore of making a hospital visit. But this seldom works, and the guilt—coupled with having to remember and stick by your alibi for years to come—

makes it hardly worth it. Better to admit you know all about your pal's calamity, and do the right thing—pay a visit.

In order to make your visit as enjoyable as possible—for both of you—it's best to observe a few basic rules. To wit:

• Call ahead, and find out what the visiting hours are. Then be sure your friend knows when you'll be stopping by. He may want to make sure things like bedpans are safely out of the picture.

• Don't bring any other friends along, unless they too know the patient, and the patient knows they're coming. For one thing, people recovering from surgery don't like surprises—they've already had plenty—and for another, they don't generally feel they're looking tip-top. So give them no cause for embarrassment.

• Ask ahead about any restrictions, before you bring flowers or food with you. Also, ask if there's anything in particular the patient would like you to bring—a current issue of a magazine, a paperback book, an audio tape.

• Wash your own hands thoroughly before and after your visit, and while you're there don't use the phone or the in-room bathroom. If you've got the flu or some such thing yourself, skip the visit altogether and just make a phone call, or send a note.

• Don't stay more than half an hour. In most cases the nurse will chase you out anyway, but even if she doesn't, you shouldn't risk tiring your friend out. While you're there, keep your conversation upbeat and optimistic, even if your friend's swaddled in a body cast from his eyebrows to his toenails.

• And just because your friend may have tubes running in and out of his nose, that doesn't mean you should take this opportunity to monopolize the conversation. Let him talk (if he can), and just listen. Sometimes, a patient needs nothing more than to just ramble on—to tell you the gory details of how he got here, what his doctors have told him, what he feels like.

Under no circumstances should you try to top him with harrowing stories of your own. This is his time to shine. One day, if things go badly, it will be yours.

"Right This Way, Please"

Such a harmless setting—a lovely restaurant, with soft lighting, white linen cloths, and a gleaming array of silver and crystal. Who would think that here, even as the violin plays and the wine is poured, a budding romance could be abruptly curtailed, or a promising career scuttled?

But it can happen. In the time it takes to brandish a gold toothpick, you can ruin a relationship, or shock a CEO looking to hire a new right-hand man. Never forget, it pays to pay attention to the finer points of dining. For instance:

• Confronted with a veritable arsenal of utensils, work from the outside in. If you're unsure at any point, sip your water until you see what your host, or someone else at the table, is using.

• Wield your cutlery in whichever way you prefer: the American style—where the fork is switched from the left hand to the right after cutting each piece of meat—or the Continental style, where the knife remains in the right hand and the fork in the left throughout the meal. Both are acceptable, though the Continental, which is actually more practical, is becoming more popular all the time.

• When spooning soup, always spoon away from yourself. When there's just a little bit left in the bowl, you may go after it by tilting the bowl away, too. One noted authority on etiquette says that it's perfectly all right to lift a consommé cup or bowl to drink off the last of the broth; to this I say, no soup is that good.

• Use your butter knife only for spreading butter. Your bread or roll should be broken with your fingers, not cut with the knife.

• When leaving the table in the middle of the meal, deposit your napkin, loosely folded, on the seat of your chair. No one wants to look at your soiled napkin while you're away.

When leaving your napkin at the end of the meal, leave it loosely folded on the table, to one side of your plate.

• When you're taking a break—if you've gone to the men's room, or if you're simply taking a breather—leave your fork and knife on your plate, spread apart, their tips angled toward the center; the tines of the fork should face down. This will tell an educated waiter that you're not done yet.

• When you are done, lay your knife across the upper right rim of your plate, with the cutting side of the blade in. Lay your fork beside it, on the inside, tines up or down.

Tipping

It's a swank restaurant, the kind of place where you actually have to make a reservation, dress well, and mind your p's and q's. It's also the kind of place where you'll be tipping all and sundry. Here's who, and how much:

The maitre d'. This is very tricky. If you're unknown in this establishment, and you can just sense that he's steering you toward Siberia (it's a hint if you have to pass through a fire door to get to your table), you might consider discreetly slipping him a ten-spot, and quietly asking "for a table in the main room."

If he just naturally gives you a good table (and for a handsome fellow like yourself, why shouldn't he?), you might reward him with that ten on your way out. Do this, especially, if you're planning to come back.

The sommelier. Remember, I said this was a swank joint. The customary tip for a knowledgeable wine steward, one who helps with your wine selection and who presents the wine to your table, is two or three dollars per bottle opened. Or, if you wish, eight percent of the total cost of the wine you order.

The waiter. The usual tip, depending on the ritziness of the restaurant, coupled with the courtesy and efficiency of the service, is 15 to 20 percent of the pre-tax bill.

The captain. At better restaurants, a tuxedoed captain will take responsibility for much of your dining experience—from taking your order to lighting your flambé. On the check, you may split the tip so that the waiter receives, say, twelve percent, and the captain eight. If you choose, you can split it down the middle—and give each one ten percent. It's up to you.

If you prefer, you may also leave the usual tip (for the waiter only) on the check, and then just give a ten, or twenty in some instances, in cash to the captain directly.

The coat-check. In some places, there is a posted charge for the coat-check. Here, it is permissible to pay only that amount (the theory being that the coat-check person is paid a living wage out of it). Or you can always be a sport and spring for an extra buck.

Under most circumstances, the idea is to tip one dollar for each item you've checked.

The doorman, and valet. If there's a doorman who hails you a cab after your meal, give him two or three dollars. If it's in the middle of a blizzard, make it four or five.

If a valet brings your car around, you'll have to pay whatever the posted valet fee is. If there isn't one, give him two or three dollars.

Table for One

Even in a life as chock full of friends as yours, you will on occasion have reason to dine alone. You looked in the larder and came up bare, you're in a strange city on a business trip, your pals are all otherwise engaged. Your first response might be to call in a pizza, but if you can't face sitting home and your cable's on the fritz, put on a clean shirt (did I really have to mention that?) and head on out.

The first thing to deal with is your fear of appearing to be a loser. (If this is a Saturday night, that fear is quin-tupled—and frankly, you might be better off staying home with the 'za.) When you approach the hostess, or whoever's doing the seating, keep your head erect, your eyes level, and your voice firm: "A table for one, please." And don't try to add some explanation or excuse ("My girlfriend's on a photo shoot this week," or "I just blew into town to wrap up a studio deal"): they're not interested, and they wouldn't believe you even if they'd been listening. To them, you're just a guy who's going to occupy a table that could have seated two people, where you'll only be spending money for one. Already they don't like you.

That's why you need to be polite but in control, and wearing that clean shirt. You don't want to give them any obvious reason for seating you in the foyer of the men's room. And if they try, you want to be able to muster some authority when you decline.

Once seated, you will want to make a quick reconnaissance of the tables around you. Are there other lonely geeks—oops, I mean "solo diners"—or is it exclusively cooing couples? The couples, of course, couldn't care less if you live or die; as for the other singles, they'll either mind their own business, or throw you a commiserating smile. If the smile comes from someone you could reasonably see spending anywhere from an hour to a lifetime with, return it. And, if you are feeling very bold, gesture at the empty chair at your own table and invite her to sit in it.

If, however, you come in alone and it looks like you're going to stay that way, take out your survival materials: a book, magazine, notepad. Dining alone without something to read, or write on, is like going over Niagara Falls without a barrel. You need some protection, something with which you can at least appear to be occupied. Do not, however, bring a newspaper, unless you're prepared to be endlessly folding it over, rustling pages, wiping the ink off your fingers.

In magazines, your choice is limited to the upscale and the arcane: *The New Yorker* is fine; so is *Media Week*. *Wrestling World* is not. Books shouldn't be too cumbersome, nor should their title or cover art call your character into question. Why do I mention this? Because on a business trip to the Midwest, I took along a perfectly respectable novel by Kingsley Amis, without noting that its title was *I Want It Now* and that its cover (which bore no relation to anything that went on in the book) showed a naked blonde sprawled across a pink satin sheet. It took me several meals before I realized why my waitresses might be treating me with something less than the usual deference.

When you are done with your meal, do not linger unduly: even if the book you brought turns out to be a spellbinder, finish it at home. And leave a generous tip. You may be back again, and even if not, you'll be enhancing the reputation of the single diner and doing a service to all those who come after you.

Toasting

You're hosting a dinner party. Your special guest is the president for life of a small, but well-heeled, nation-state with which you, or your company, has enjoyed a remarkably rewarding business relationship. (Oh, if only those pesky human-rights people would stop raising such a fuss!) You wish to honor him with a toast. How do you properly go about it?

First, look around the table to make sure everyone is seated, and that everyone has a glass of something in front of them. Wine or champagne is customary, but even water is fine. All that counts is it's liquid.

Get the attention of your guests. The easiest way to do this is by rising from your chair. If you prefer, you may remain seated and gently tap a spoon against the side of your glass.

Face the guest of honor as you speak, but also be sure to include the other people at the table in your gaze.

Although a toast can be offered at the midway point or the conclusion of the meal, perhaps the best time to do it is right at the beginning. (This way you'll be able to relax and enjoy the rest of the evening.) "Your Excellency," you say, holding your glass in your right hand, "it is with great pleasure that we welcome you to America, a nation that shares with yours a profound and abiding respect for life, liberty, and heretofore unexploited mineral resources. May your sojourn here prove both enjoyable and mutually productive." Raising your glass in the air: "To His Excellency, Fugazio von Vega!" Take a sip, not a swig, and sit down.

Time elapsed? No more than a minute. Most toasts should not exceed thirty seconds.

If you happen to know what the traditional salutation is in Fugazio's native tongue, it is nice to use it just before everyone drinks. If not, you can always resort to one of the usual terms, such as "*Prosit*," "*Skoal*," "*À Votre Santé*," or "*Cheers*." It is not necessary, or advised, for you, or your guests, to clink glasses after the toast.

But suppose your guest chooses to toast you in return? Sit modestly, hands in your lap, and accept the praise. When everyone else drinks, you don't. (It would be like that curious Russian custom of clapping for yourself.) Just nod to Fugazio, and say "Thank you so much," and smile at your tablemates.

CHAPTER VI

On Holiday

—◆◆◆—

"To travel hopefully is a better thing than to arrive."

—ROBERT LOUIS STEVENSON,
Viginibus Puerisque (1881)

Hotel Living

Twenty-four-hour room service, fresh towels twice a day, a chocolate on your pillow each night—is there anything that can beat life at a good hotel?

Still, many travelers try to economize. "Who's gonna be in the room? We'll be out seeing the sights!" True. But you're also going to be getting up in the morning, going to bed at night, sleeping, sometimes eating, and often relaxing at your hotel. It's your home away from home—it ought to be at least as nice as the one you left.

When checking in, be sure to ask about the location of the room. Does it have a view? What's the view of? (The parking lot doesn't qualify.) Does it face onto a noisy street— or a quiet back garden? Is it right next to the elevator bank? (If there's a convention going on, you will definitely want to move farther away from the elevator shaft.) Finally, take a look at the room—and before you let the bellman go, decide if you want to stay in it. If not, call down to the desk and say you want to see another room that's available. (Although it makes almost no sense, many hotels will hang on to their better rooms, in case the president—or simply a more particular guest—arrives. *You* should be that particular guest.)

If you're going to be staying in the room for more than a night, make it your own. Unpack your bag completely (your clothes will thank you) and stash the bag in the closet. Arrange your toiletries on the shelf in the bathroom, tune the radio to a station you like, and adjust the thermostat. Find out if there's a free overnight shoe-polishing service (increasingly common these days) and take advantage of it; personally, I always bring my dirty shoes on trips with me now.

If some of your clothes have gotten wrinkled in transit, particularly suits, hang them on the back of the bathroom door, turn on a hot shower, and leave them in there to soak up the steam for ten or fifteen minutes. Don't do this if you need to wear that suit right away; it might need time to cool down and dry out.

Stay off the phone until you've carefully read the little card stuck beside or under it; this will tell you what, if any, charges the hotel adds on for calls made from the room. For a while, hotels were getting rich with these surcharges; then there was a rebellion, and they cut back. Still, it's better to check before dialing—and use whatever phone card you carry.

When ordering room service, leave ample time for delivery. And try not to be in the shower, or on an important phone call, when it arrives. Figure out in advance where you'll want to eat it (on the balcony? the bed? at the desk?) so you can tell the server. Ascertain if the tip is included or not (the check you sign will usually say), and when you're done eating, either call down to room service to tell them to come up and clear everything away, or put the tray, or cart, into the hall yourself. (Even then, call downstairs to let them know it's there.) Otherwise, your room will start to smell of leftover fries and cold coffee.

When it's time to check out, call the front desk as soon as you know you won't be adding any other charges (breakfast, phone calls, etc.) to your bill; even if you won't actually be leaving for another hour or two, tell them you'll be down shortly. Or, if you'd like to look the bill over first, ask them to send it up. (On my last visit to New York, I discovered that someone had enjoyed a positively monstrous breakfast and charged it to my room.) Either way, you won't wind up standing at the front desk while the clerk waits for the printout and your cab idles at the curb.

Handouts

When you're traveling, sometimes it seems like every hand you see is stretched out, palm up . . . waiting. You start to feel like a cash machine, to which the entire world has the secret number. But what's the alternative, short of never going anywhere?

Before setting out, make sure you have plenty of small bills in your pocket—mostly ones, but a couple of fives too.

At the airport or train station, tip the porter or skycap a buck for each bag you entrust to his care.

At your hotel, you don't need to tip the doorman who ushers you in, or the valet (if you drove there) who puts your car away. Valets are tipped only when they return a car to you—a buck is customary. (But if you go to an unfamiliar restaurant, particularly in California, do be forewarned: many times there's a posted valet charge ranging anywhere from two to four dollars.)

The bellhop who brings your bags upstairs gets a buck a bag.

The hotel personnel who do you small and sundry favors—like bringing up a load of hangers or an extra pillow—get a buck or two, depending on the task and how well it's been done.

The waiter who wheels in your room-service cart usually gets a fifteen percent tip, which you can write on the check. But read the fine print on the bill: the hotel may have already added on a "gratuity." If they have, you don't have to. If, however, they've only added on a "room service charge," you should still add a tip: room service charges don't go to the waiter, they go to the hotel.

If there's a concierge, and you call upon him (to get you play tickets, a dinner reservation at a chichi restaurant, directions to an out-of-the-way spot) five or ten dollars would be about right.

If, while you're in town, you take a guided bus tour of the local sights, you might consider tipping the guide anywhere from two to five dollars, especially if he or she answered a couple of your questions.

At the end of your stay, you should leave a tip for the chambermaids. A dollar a night is the usual, but if you're staying at the Ritz, you may want to raise it to two. Simply leave the bills (not change) on the bedside table, anchored by the lamp or ashtray.

If it's a small bed-and-breakfast place, the kind where the owner himself slices your muffin and makes your bed, you can skip the tip. If it's more of an inn or country hotel, you can slip fifteen percent of your total bill into an envelope and leave it with the owner at the end of your stay; he'll parcel it out among the housekeepers and kitchen help.

Leaving a hotel, you should tip the guy who comes for your luggage (again, a buck a bag), and the doorman, too, if he turns out to be the one who helps load them into the cab (a dollar or two). Tip the cabbie (ten percent of the fare) who drives you to the airport, and give the same to the cabbie who drives you home from the airport. If there's someone there to greet you at your door, chances are she'd prefer a kiss. (If she doesn't, you may want to hang on to the cab.)

Two for the Road

You're mad about each other in the city, can't wait to get behind closed doors, love to linger in bed on a Sunday morning. So what could go wrong on vacation?

A good deal. Be advised that traveling together, whether it's on a package tour of Europe, or a week on a sun-drenched beach, is an altogether different situation, and one fraught with fresh perils.

For one thing, do try to pick, if possible, a place to go where neither one of you has already planted a bumper crop of memories. If you and an old girlfriend always spent your summers on Cape Cod, you might consider Florida with your new flame. Better for her, better for you.

Keep in mind something else, too: on vacation, the two of you are now deprived of your private living spaces, and your privacy. Even if you're married, you are now confined to one room, with a bathroom to share, and a TV that may receive only two fuzzy channels. Give each other some space—read on the terrace while your companion calls home. If you're hungry and she's not, order up your own room service, and let her do the same after she works up an appetite.

Even when you leave the hotel, allow for some individual plans. No two people have exactly the same interests, and compromise isn't always the wisest solution. Why should she accompany you to the folklore show, just so you can return the favor by sitting through a performance of Wagner's *Ring*? Go your separate ways—and you'll have something interesting to tell each other about later.

Don't try to do *everything*. The purpose of a vacation is to relax and slow down, and just because you're in Rome for only five days doesn't mean you have to see, do, tour, and taste everything the place has to offer. It's called The Eternal City—it'll be there the next time you visit.

If you have some old friends in the area, don't assume you can simply call them at the last minute from your hotel and have them drop everything to come and see you (or worse, show you around). You're on vacation, they're not. It's better, all around, to drop them a note before you leave home, letting them know where you'll be staying (not at their house) and even what night you might like to meet for dinner. If the woman you're traveling with is not the same one they last saw you with, you might forewarn them of that: "I'm so eager for you to meet Ingrid, the prima ballerina I met in Copenhagen." This will give your male friends a chance to bite their knuckles, in private, before you all get together.

The Perfect Houseguest

Sometimes—though far less often than might be expected—you will be invited to a friend's house for the weekend, or longer. Assuming you like this person, and the house has indoor plumbing, here's what to remember when you go:

• A gift for your host and/or hostess. Ideally, bring something they can use and enjoy that weekend—wine, food that needs no further preparation (chocolate truffles, an exotic coffee blend, a basket of fresh fruit), CDs they might like to listen to, books they'd like to read.

• Try, also, to bring most of what you know you'll need. If you can manage it, you might pack a few towels (especially beach towels) that they won't then have to supply and launder. Bring all the socks, underwear, swimsuits, etc., you'll require; do not plan on running a quick load in their washing machine.

• As much as possible, fall into the schedule and rhythm of your hosts. If they have their breakfast at 8:30 (an hour before you're usually awake), set a travel alarm and get up in time. If they go to bed at 10 (two hours before you usually do), go to bed; if you can't sleep, read quietly. Do not prowl the halls at night like a ghost, banging into doorknobs and making the floorboards creak.

• Do not, in fact, prowl the halls at any time. Just because you're a houseguest, that doesn't mean you've been offered the run of the place. Unless expressly invited, stay clear of the host's private quarters, other guests' rooms, closed closets, etc. Do not inspect their medicine cabinets; if you need something, ask for it.

• Stay as long as you were invited to stay, and no longer. Even if your hosts are staying on in the house, and your room appears to you to be unaccounted for, don't assume you can linger there. They may have other plans, and they may just want to spend some time by themselves. Yours is not to reason why, yours is but to thank them and fly.

· Back home, send a thank-you note and, if you wish, a small gift (flowers, for instance). Do not ask if you can book the same room for a week in August.

Packing It All In

You know the advantages of traveling light. And you know the difficulties of trekking through airports with bags suspended from every limb and dragging at your feet. So this time, approach packing for a trip with fresh vision and resolve.

The Bag

By now you know that heavy-duty nylon bags are stronger, lighter, and less expensive than the old-fashioned hard-sided luggage. They are also less likely to tear than canvas or vinyl, and Lord knows they can't get dented. Furthermore, they are less likely to get stolen at the airport; thieves like leather— particularly when it's Gucci or Vuitton—because even if the contents turn out to be disappointing, they've still got a nice bag to show for their day's work.

On planes, these nylon bags are also easier to wedge under your seat or into the overhead compartment.

For suits and coats and things that you need to keep from being wrinkled or crushed, use a garment bag. But get one that has (a) a comfortable shoulder strap, (b) a simple spine across the top rather than an elaborate hard frame (which makes it difficult to hang or fold), and (c) a permanently attached hook on top—you don't want to be fumbling to attach a hook while everyone else waiting to board the plane is looking for a noose to hang you with.

Put a plastic name tag on every bag you bring; those little paper tags that you get out of the basket at the check-in desk are too easily torn off. And if your bags are fairly generic in appearance, consider slapping a bold decal, or some other identifying marker, on them. It's not just to help you spot them on the luggage carousel; it's to keep somebody else from mistakenly walking off with yours.

And throw one of your business cards into the bag, too—on top of your clothes. If the tag gets torn off, and the bag goes to Sumatra, there's still a chance it will find its way home this way.

On Checking Luggage

The general wisdom is to avoid it at all costs. But if you're not going to be making tight connections, your bags are heavy, or your back is bad, go ahead. Just make sure you check in early, and that you see your bags have been correctly tagged by the check-in clerk. Your carry-on bag should contain toiletries, a change of underwear and a fresh shirt—just in case your checked bags do go to Sumatra . . . (see *The Contents* following).

The Contents

When packing for a trip, ask yourself this: am I going to a place where there are no laundries? If that's the case, pack lots of stuff. But if it's not, you can safely limit yourself to three or four days' worth of socks, underwear, shirts. True, hotels charge plenty for the service, but there's something to be said for having things cleaned professionally, and so conveniently.

The alternative—the in-room method—is unquestionably cheaper. A stoppered sink, a pack of Woolite, and a shower rod is all you need. But—and I speak from experience—somehow your things *look* like you washed them yourself. They're wrinkled, they smell of Woolite, and quite often, when you have no other choice but to wear them, they're still damp.

When selecting what to bring, think monochromatic. Try to coordinate everything around navy blue, for instance; keep your accessories, shoes, ties, all revolving around one or two colors (preferably dark, muted, and solid). Save the paisleys and plaids for home. This way you can pack fewer things, and if one item gets soiled, you've got a ready replacement.

To save space, stuff your socks and rolled-up belts in your shoes. Don't put your toiletries into one of those firm leather kits, which resist being shmushed, but into a plastic bag with a drawstring top. Use small refillable plastic bottles to take only as much shampoo, moisturizer, sunscreen, etc., as you'll need (and do keep in mind that nearly all respectable hotels provide many of these things in the room now). If, however, you're bringing your favorite cologne, leave it in the glass bottle it came in; plastic can alter its scent.

Also, be sure to take these toiletries in the carry-on bag that never leaves your side; for one thing, you won't risk losing important medications you may be taking along, and for another you won't risk a shampoo bottle exploding all over the Harris tweed you so lovingly packed. (Note: Leave a little air in your liquid containers; otherwise, the lowered air pressure in the plane may cause them to spring a leak.)

And finally, leave a fully loaded toiletries bag in your bathroom cabinet at home at all times. When you have to

take a sudden and unexpected excursion, it's easy to forget
your razor, your shaving cream, your dental floss. Better to
keep them all together, and ready to go when you are.

Airborne

To fly through the air with the greatest of ease, there are a
number of small, but useful, steps to take in advance.

• Put your wallet in your breast pocket, or in one of
those zippered pouches that fit on your belt. You'll find it's
much easier to fish out the money for your headphones, and
you won't get off the plane five hours later with the imprint
of your wallet permanently affixed to your buttocks.

One caveat: if you're wearing that zippered pouch, and
a comely young woman sits down beside you, conceal it at all
costs. Convenient as it is, it's also uncontestably doofy—even
more so than a wheeled baggage cart.

• Wear a watch you can easily reset to new time zones. I,
for instance, have a fancy quartz model, which has defied
jewelers in three cities; no one knows how to reset it. The old-
fashioned stem, wind-up kind is much simpler. Your travel
alarm clock should also be dependably low-tech (never ever
rely solely on your hotel wake-up call).

• If you have a problem breathing all that stale, recycled
cabin air (and who doesn't?), consider asking, when you
book your ticket, what kind of plane it is. In a *Consumer
Reports* survey, airplanes varied greatly in the air quality they
delivered—one of the worst, for instance, was the Boeing 757
(poor ventilation and cramped seat configuration), while the
Boeing 747-400 was the best.

• The cabin air can dry out soft contact lenses and make them uncomfortable to wear. Either take them out, or bring along some lubricating drops. Even if you don't wear contacts, you might find that eye drops are a help on long flights.

If the plane makes a stopover, you can always get off for a short while. The ventilation on grounded planes is even worse than when they're in the air.

• If you're flying with a cold (something you should avoid whenever possible) consult your doctor and take some sort of decongestant before boarding the plane. You might also carry a mentholated inhaler to expand your nasal passages on the descent. And try not to fall asleep on the plane, particularly during the last half hour; when you're asleep, you swallow less often (which allows the pressure to build up), and you won't be aware of the increasing discomfort until you wake up—feeling miserable.

• If you're feeling okay, and it's just popping your ears that you need to do, you can try the unattractive, but generally effective, Valsalva maneuver. (Scuba divers do it.) Pinching your nostrils shut and closing your mouth, blow air into your cheeks—gradually—until you feel your ears unplug. If only one side pops, loosen up on the nostril on that side and try the maneuver again. But as even this method can, theoretically, damage the ear, use it sensibly and don't blow hard enough to take the top off Mt. St. Helens.

• Choose your seat with care. Aisle seats, of course, offer the advantages of added leg room and the chance to get up without crawling over other people. Window seats provide a view, a whiff of privacy, and a headrest (the spot between the cabin wall and the top of your seat) where you can wedge a pillow and try to sleep. The vibrations from the plane, however, will make that tough.

Middle seats, believe it or not, have a fraction more luggage space underneath them. This in no way compensates for how awful they are in every other respect.

For the smoothest ride, ask for a seat over the wing. The bumpiest seats are the ones in back. To get off early, sit up front. To stretch out over several seats and sleep (on, say, the red-eye to Los Angeles), move to the rear.

• ECS (Economy Class Syndrome) is an actual condition written up in the British medical journal, *The Lancet*; it can show up even weeks after a flight, and includes everything from minor aches and pains to shortness of breath, heart attacks, and strokes. It all has to do with the cramped quarters, the dehydration, and the lousy air endured on board the plane.

To avoid ECS, drink no alcohol during the flight. Do drink lots of water. Take aspirin to thin the blood, and do whatever stretching and exercising you can do on board without alarming your fellow passengers. Weight training is clearly out, but it's easy enough to reach your arms up toward the overhead light, to arch your back and twist your feet on the floor, or to take a leisurely stroll to the back of the plane. Back there, there's sometimes enough room to do toe touches. Just watch out for the meals cart.

Out of Sync

Jet lag has been with us for as long as there have been jets. And like the common cold, jet lag has yet to be cured . . . though some progress has been made.

In one recent study at MIT, young men given a pill containing melatonin, the body's own sleep-inducing hormone, dropped off to sleep in five or six minutes. Just think how rapidly this kind of drug could readjust your normal circadian (twenty-four-hour) rhythm. At the moment, the FDA has yet to approve any melatonin drug, but the stuff is available in capsule form at most health food stores; the usual dosage is 5 to 10 mg, taken anywhere from 30 to 90 minutes before bedtime in your new destination. (But as with any such drug, ask your physician first before trying it out.)

In the meantime, you just have to fall back on some of the tried-and-true methods for dealing with jet lag.

Perhaps the most important ingredient in beating jet lag is light; your body and brain take many of their cues from their exposure to light and dark. That's why, if you should fly from the U.S. to Europe, and arrive at, say, 9 A.M., it might be a good idea to get out and about in the morning light. But these timings can be tricky, and much depends on your usual sleep schedule, what time zone you flew in from, etc. If you want a chart to help you figure out when to draw the curtains and when to bask in sun, or artificial light, you can pick up a book called *How to Beat Jet Lag: A Practical Guide for Air Travelers* (written by several sleep researchers—Daniel Oren, Walter Reich, Norman Rosenthal, and Thomas Wehr). Just select a direction and a distance, and the book will suggest an optimal schedule for you.

Or you can call a company called Circadian Travel Technologies (1-800-621-5483) and order one of their Jet-Lag calculators; for $9.95, it'll tell you when to avoid light, and when to seek it out, on any trip.

What else can you do?

Try to schedule an appropriate flight—one, for instance, that leaves at a time you would normally be wide awake, and that arrives at your destination at a time when folks are still up and about. If your plane gets in, say, in the early evening, that's good—you can stay up just a few hours, then retire when everyone else does and let sleep knit up the raveled sleeve of care.

As far as your diet goes, try eating high-protein breakfasts both before and after you arrive (to get your energy up during the day) and heavy carbohydrate dinners (which, after an initial surge, will make you drowsy).

Cut out alcohol; some studies suggest it interferes with the body's ability to regulate itself. And don't smoke.

Go with the flow. Reset your own internal clock by entering into the life and schedule of the place you're at; don't keep trying to figure out what time it is back in Des Moines and what you'd be doing if you were only still at home. When in Rome, eat when the Romans do.

Stay active during the active times of day—in fact, exaggerate your activities, if possible. Sightsee, shop, hike, swim—get some exercise. And then, when night falls, try to fall asleep when everyone else does. Even if you can't, just lie there and relax. Your brain may eventually get bored enough to click off.

The Working Vacation

For starters, there's no such thing—if you're working, you're not on vacation. The whole idea of a vacation is to get away from work, not to take it with you wherever you go. A working vacation is a contradiction in terms.

Still . . . if you must, there are a few steps you can take to minimize the damage to your holiday.

If you'll be taking your laptop with you, your first

priority will be keeping it safe. While in transit, you might want to consider taking it out of its fancy carrying case—an advertisement to thieves everywhere—and put it instead in a nylon bookbag, or something inconspicuous. Your modem, mouse, etc., can be tucked into separate drawstring pouches, and you can even pad the sides of the bag with underwear and socks to absorb shocks.

Try to avoid putting the laptop in the overhead bin; it can shift around in flight, and you never know when some clod is going to throw his leaky box of live Maine lobsters on top of it. Keep it under the seat in front of you. Also, leave a disk (with a copy of your files on it) at home, and affix a clear label with your name, address, and phone number, to the laptop itself.

At your destination, book a suite, rather than a room. The idea is to have a place where you can do your work, comfortably, without turning the whole place into a make-shift office. If all you've got is a single room, then reserve the table by the window, and if the room doesn't have a comfortable work chair (most don't), request one.

And by the way, did you ask at the front desk what services the hotel might provide for doing business away from home? Some actually have small office cubicles tucked away; others have rentable computers, copiers, and type-writers; nearly all have fax services available (though the per-page prices are generally steep).

Most of the time, you're better off getting your work done early in the day; if you get on a schedule of working, say, from 9:30 to noon, you then have a chance of putting it out of your mind for the rest of the day and concentrating on having some fun. An alternative to this, however, is to reserve those hours of the day that are the least pleasant wherever you are. If, for instance, you're in a climate where only mad dogs and Englishmen go out in the afternoon, make those the hours when you hunker down with the air conditioning and crank out the work.

Finally, if you're lucky enough to be vacationing with someone, don't drone on about your work. Your companion shouldn't be penalized just because you're a workaholic. It's enough that she had to run out at 8 A.M. to get you fresh batteries for the computer. (You should always replace 'em, by the way, before you leave home.) If, over a candlelit dinner, you so much as mention your boss, your secretary, or the latest office snafu, she is entitled to take the little umbrella out of her drink and stab you with it.

Travelin' Right

Before Leaving the House

· Call your airline and your hotel to confirm your reservations. (Some of these places regard a booking more as a wish than an obligation.)

· Ask the hotel if they provide in-room robes, blow-dryers, standard toiletries, disposable slippers, etc. Anything you don't have to pack is a boon.

· Go from room to room, making sure things such as air conditioners and coffee makers are turned off. Windows closed and locked. Taps turned off. (On the way to the airport, you will still wonder whether you checked the stove, but it will be a comfort to know you made a systematic inspection.)

· Make sure the plants are watered. (See "The Green Indoors.")

• Tell your neighbor (if he's trustworthy) that you'll be away. Give him a number where you can be reached.

• If you're going anywhere exotic, check with your doctor about vaccinations, necessary medicines, etc. If he says, "Oh—well, if you're going *there*, you'd better come in for an hour or two on Tuesday," change your plans.

• Unless you plan to call in to your answering machine regularly, you might leave a new message saying you're out of town. This does, of course, advertise an empty house—but what are the chances a burglar is going to be calling in? And if you happen to be going overseas, the nuisance—and expense—of reaching your machine each night could prove sizeable.

In Transit

• Carry a pill case in your pocket with at least a day's dosage of any medication you might need.

• Leave plenty of time for getting to the airport or train station. What would you be doing with that extra half hour at home, anyway? Reading the paper, probably. Read it at the airport and cut down on your stress.

• If you suffer from hypoglycemia, sudden starvation attacks, dry throat, etc., bring with you a couple of cookies, a granola bar, a small bottle of Evian. On planes, you can sit for hours before the food service begins; on Amtrak, you'd sooner starve than eat what they're selling.

• Bring only enough reading material to get you through the trip. Do not carry heavy hardcovers. Paperbacks were invented for travel. And magazines can be discarded after you've finished reading them.

If you do bring a book, be sure its cover and title are not the kind of thing you'll be embarrassed to leave on your seat for a moment. If you were ever planning to read Stephen Hawking's *A Brief History of Time*, this is it.

• Brush up on your destination. If it's an American city you're flying to, you might even—shocking though this is—read the in-flight magazine. It's often got an article or two on local sights, restaurants, amusements. And it's yours to take—free!

• If you're heading to a foreign country, use this time to bone up on the currency conversion charts, a little local history, and a few important phrases ("Where is the bathroom?" "How much does that cost?" "Why is everyone running the other way?").

On Arrival

• Announce your destination—hotel, office building, whatever—clearly and with authority to the driver of the bus, cab, or van. For one, you want to know right now if you're getting on the wrong conveyance. Two, you want to give the impression you've been here before (so you don't get taken on the scenic route getting there).

• If it's a foreign country, have the address you're going to written out, so you can show it to the driver. You don't want your pronunciation to land you on the wrong side of the river.

• If possible, try not to schedule the first things you have to do too close to the time of your arrival. Not only is travel a very "fluid" proposition—you could be sitting on the tarmac while the opera curtain rises—it's nice to have a few hours to acclimate yourself.

• If you have business appointments the next day, be sure to ask at your hotel how long it will take to get there, what the best route is, and if there are any problems—such as bridge construction, or huge conventions in the same area—that you should know about.

• In foreign lands, be sure to keep some local currency with you when you head back to the airport. There are departure taxes to pay, and sometimes they can't be paid in American dollars. Ask ahead of time.

Homecoming

• If you are still carrying foreign currency, change it back to American at the airport. Sure, you might get a better rate in the city, and yes, there's always the chance you'll be going back to Zamburnia, but more likely than not these smudged coins and colorful bills will turn up, six years from now, at the bottom of a desk drawer. And by then, Zamburnia will have been annexed by Yaboobistan.

• Before retrieving all your phone calls, have a piece of paper handy to jot them down on—and answer them all the next day. Open your mail at once—I once didn't and I missed the date of a lecture (a *paid* lecture!) I was supposed to give.

• Open the windows, water the plants, pick up any pets you might have left in the care of friends.

• Give a small gift to any friend who cared for a pet. If the pet is anything exotic or difficult (say, a boa constrictor), make it a large gift.

· Get your photos developed, look them over, have a chuckle or two, then put them back in the envelope, put the envelope in a drawer, and never again mention them to anyone.

Next Trip

· No matter how much you enjoyed your vacation, think long and hard before booking another trip there. The world is a big place, with many wonderful spots—don't you want to see as many of them as you can? And consider, too, how fragile a happy memory is—do you really want to risk ruining this one with a return trip? (What are the chances that you'll meet another slumming model who begs you to remove the sea urchin spines from her foot? Not good, my friend, not good.)

CHAPTER VII

At Ease

"Manners makyth man."
—Winchester College motto

Poker Politesse

Of all the card games played, poker is undoubtedly the most popular and democratic—if you have never once been invited to join a game of seven-card stud, or Texas Hold 'em, you have not yet been truly initiated into the male fraternity.

To explain the rules of each variation of the game would be beyond the purview of this book; whole volumes have been written on such stuff. But to enumerate some of the fundamental rules of table etiquette is not. (Many of these guidelines, incidentally, hold true for other card games, too.) So, the next time you pull up a chair to play, remember to:

• *Act in turn.* The action in a poker game proceeds clockwise around the table, one player at a time. It's not only the polite way to play—it's the only fair way to play. If, for instance, you act out of turn and discard your hand, you've just told players who should have acted ahead of you that it's now safer to bluff. Which isn't fair, either, to others who may have already chosen to fold.

• *Ante up neatly.* If you toss your chips or money into the pot—a practice known as "splashing the pot"—you not only mess up the table, but you make it hard for others to determine if you've put in the proper amount.

• *Stay alert.* If it's your turn, and you have to stop to ask everyone what the bet is, you're slowing up the game. If you're still in the hand, stay awake.

• *If you're not in the hand, just sit quietly.* Do not talk about the cards you threw away (this can help some players, and hurt others), and do not distract the players at the table with chitchat. They've still got money at stake.

• *Bluff, but never lie.* Bluffing is a strategic technique in which you bet or raise on a hand unlikely to be the best at the table. It's a fair and square part of the game. Lying—which is to say out loud something untrue about your hand—is not. For one thing, you shouldn't be blathering at all; to blather deceitfully is enough to get you barred from future games.

• *Settle your debts.* Don't ever bet more than you can afford to lose—and if you lose it, don't promise to pay up later. Pay up on the spot. Other players should not have to become debt collectors. (*This is in no way an endorsement of gambling.)

• *Be generous and hospitable.* If the game is regularly held at someone else's house, bring some food or drink. If it's a moveable game, offer your own place now and then (even if it means hiring a cleaning service the day before).

Cat Naps

It's four in the afternoon. The shadows are lengthening. Your eyelids are fluttering. A soft fuzz is starting to envelop your brain. What do you do? Do you force yourself to rally, to fight off the torpor with a jolt of coffee and a candy bar?

Or do you pull in at Nature's little rest stop?

More and more, sleep scientists are in agreement on this one: you ought to give up your guilt—who said it's a sin to snooze for a few minutes?—and give in to that impulse to close your eyes and drift off for a while. According to the National Commission on Sleep Disorders Research, a third of the American population suffers from chronic or periodic sleep disorders—and napping, despite its bad rep, can help.

But it has to be done right.

For optimal value, napping should be done in the mid- to late afternoon. That's when the body customarily needs it the most.

How much does the body need? Twenty minutes, at the very most an hour, is about right. Although napping is a very individual kind of thing, for most people this amount of time is right. Less, and you won't have had time to derive the restorative benefits of a nap; more, and you'll start to interfere with your nocturnal sleep patterns.

If you're at work, and you can manage it at all, close your office door, turn the ringer off on your telephone, and let your voice mail catch your calls. You might even take off your shoes, flip over an empty wastebasket, and put your feet up. Tell yourself it's for the good of the company: you'll be refreshed, and work even harder, when you wake up.

If you're at home, it's easy—but for a nap to qualify as a nap, and not serious sleeping, you must:

• Stay dressed. Once you take off your pants, or put on pj's, you're not napping—you're turning in.

• Cover yourself with a newspaper or magazine, spread across your chest. Blankets are out—too much like "real sleeping."

• Curl up on a sofa, easy chair, or chaise. Not the bed. If you start retiring to the bedroom to rest at other times than at night, you risk eroding the singular purpose of the room—nocturnal sleep—which can further disturb your normal sleep patterns.

• Get up within the allotted time. Make sure your shoes are tied, your belt's buckled, and your hair's in place. Then sally forth into the world again. If anyone asks where you were, say you were meditating.

Loosely defined, you were.

Cheers

Even in an age as abstemious as ours, when some people insist on drinking nothing but water from glacial moraines, it's a good idea to know your way around the standard bar setup, and to have the bare essentials in your own home. What do these include?

For starters, you need a cabinet, a counter space, or at least a couple of shelves where you can keep your paraphernalia all together. How smooth can you look rummaging through your pot holder drawer, looking for a leftover swizzle stick?

Next, you need an assortment of basic implements:

A jigger—one that's marked for half- and quarter-ounces

A corkscrew
A can and bottle opener
A shaker, glass or metal, with a long spoon for stirring
An ice bucket and tongs
A paring knife, for cutting fruit peels
A good-sized pitcher, easy for pouring
A set of measuring spoons
Cocktail napkins
A couple of small bowls, suitable for nuts or olives
A set of coasters (and not the sort that feature the
    Hooter girls, 1995)

You can certainly get fancy, and add strainers and squeezers and muddlers (for mashing up mint and herbs), but I assume you have no intentions of opening your bar to the public at large.

Next comes glassware. You need an assortment, in matching pairs or more. Tumblers, for drinks such as gin and tonic; champagne flutes; wine glasses; brandy snifters; martini glasses; beer steins; and old-fashioned glasses, which, in a pinch, can stand in for other things.

As for the liquor itself, a few staples should suffice: a good bottle of red wine and a dry white; a chilled champagne.

Vodka, gin, Scotch, bourbon, vermouth, rum.

Also, brandy, for those late-night interludes, on a bearskin rug, by a roaring fire. For the record (as there is sometimes confusion on this score), cognac, famed for its smooth and dry aroma, is brandy produced in the Cognac region of France. So while all cognac is brandy, not all brandy is cognac.

Armagnac is also a brandy. Even drier than cognac, it is produced in the Armagnac (no surprise) region of France.

And although both wine and brandy start out as grape juice, the length of time they've spent in the bottle is relevant only to wine; brandy ages only while it's in the wooden cask, and stops the minute it's bottled. So if you buy an 1860 vintage that was bottled in 1864, for all practical purposes it's still only four years old. That's one reason you seldom see a vintage year noted on a cognac bottle.

You might also lay in a bottle or two of cordials (also known as liqueurs). Depending on your taste, and the taste of your friends, you might want to keep in stock some Amaretto (almond-flavored), Curacao (orange-flavored), Dubonnet (a French aperitif), or Peppermint Schnapps.

For friends who request something snazzy, one of those drinks with names like Dixie Julep or Brandy Sangaree, keep a bartender's guide on hand. Or invite them to prepare it themselves, just the way they like it.

And, of course, keep the ice bucket filled.

Mixing Things Up

If you're going to offer your guests mixed drinks, you're going to have to measure some things. Now, don't panic—this isn't chemistry class all over again. But there are a few things you should know.

A jigger is 1½ ounces.
A pony is 1 ounce.
A bar spoon is ½ teaspoon.
A dash is 7 to 10 drops.

In nearly every case, ice is your first ingredient. It can come in cubes, crushed, cracked, or shaved, but always put it in the glass, or shaker, first; that way, the liquids are chilled as you pour them over the ice, and you cut down on the splashing that would occur if you tried to plop the ice in later. For the record, most on-the-rocks cocktails, including high-balls and old-fashioneds, take cubes. When stirring or shaking cocktails, use cubes or cracked ice. If you're getting very fancy, whipping up frappes and tall drinks that require straws and umbrellas, use shaved or crushed ice.

It's a nice touch, too, if you pre-chill the glasses. If the fridge is too full for that, then just fill the glasses with ice for a few minutes beforehand. For "frosted" glasses, stash them in the freezer, or tuck them under a blanket of crushed ice.

Some drinks you shake, some you stir. Stir drinks made up of clear liquors and other ingredients; if it contains a carbonated mixer (ginger ale, Coke, tonic water) stir gently, so you don't kill off the effervescence. But keep the stirring within limits: too little and things won't get mixed properly, too much and you melt the ice, thereby diluting the drink.

Shaking—briskly—is usually a good idea for drinks containing fruit juices, eggs, sugar, or cream; if you're making up a punch, a sour, or some frothy concoction, save yourself some trouble and use the blender.

And speaking of fruit juices—use fresh. If the drink calls for a twist of lemon, lime, or orange, wash the outside of the fruit first. Then peel off a strip about an inch and a half long and a quarter-inch wide; give it a twist over the glass, to extract that drop of oil, then drop it into the glass.

Finally, if you're making up a batch of one cocktail that several people are going to share, and you want to make sure everybody gets the same quality and amount, line up their empty glasses: fill each one halfway, then go back to the beginning and top them off.

Common Libations

While there are hundreds, possibly thousands, of cocktail combinations, there are a handful that should figure in any cultivated man's bar repertoire. These include:

The Screwdriver. Put several ice cubes into a tall glass; pour in 2 oz. of vodka, then fill the rest of the glass with fresh orange juice. Stir.

The Bloody Mary. Shake or stir the following ingredients: 1½ oz. vodka, 3 oz. tomato juice, a dash of lemon juice, a dash of Worcestershire sauce, two or three drops of Tabasco sauce, a pinch of salt and pepper. Serve over ice cubes, with a wedge of lime.

To make a Bullshot, substitute chilled beef bouillon for the tomato juice.

Gin and tonic. Just what it sounds like—pour 2 oz. of gin, over ice cubes, into a tall glass. Then add the tonic, or quinine, water.

Manhattan. Stir with cracked ice 1½ oz. whiskey, ¾ oz. sweet vermouth, and a dash of angostura bitters—then serve it up straight, or over ice, with a maraschino cherry. If you want it drier, use dry vermouth instead, and serve it with an olive.

Seven & Seven. Over ice, pour 1½ oz. Seagram's whiskey, then top it off with 7-Up.

Black Russian. Stir 1½ oz. vodka and ¾ oz. Kahlua, then pour over ice cubes into an old-fashioned cocktail glass.

Margarita. Shake with cracked ice 1½ oz. tequila, ½ oz. Cointreau or Triple Sec, and the juice of half a lime. Strain and serve into a chilled glass, the rim of which you have rubbed with lemon or lime rind and dipped in salt.

The Martini. In some ways, this is the aristocrat of cocktails, with more variations than you can shake a swizzle stick at. But the classic goes like this: into your pitcher, brimming with dry, hard-frozen ice, stir 1½ oz. of dry gin and ¾ oz. of dry vermouth. (This is the original 2:1 ratio of gin to vermouth; for "drier" martinis, increase that ratio to 3:1, or 5:1.) But do put the gin in first, then the vermouth; the gin should "smoke" as you pour it in over the ice. Stir it briskly to make sure it's cold, then strain and serve it—straight up in a chilled and stemmed cocktail glass. Add an olive, if you like. If you'd like to make what's called a Gibson, make the martini extra dry and toss in a couple of pearl onions.

Serving Wine

Sometimes it seems like there are so many rules and regulations about wine that it's safer just to drink beer. When to drink it, how to drink it, what temperature to serve it at, which year is the best, which year is the pits. The mystique is so thick you're afraid to buy or serve anything with a cork. (At least with a screw-top jug, you know exactly what you're getting.)

But it doesn't have to be that way.

Wine is just fermented juice, stuck in a bottle with a fancy label. Don't allow yourself to be cowed by it. Drink what you like, the way you like it, accompanied by whatever you enjoy it with.

That said, there *are* some general guidelines which may increase your enjoyment of the stuff. To wit:

When it comes to red table wines, they're best served at room temperature—which, by the way, means 65 to 68 degrees. That's actually a little cooler than most rooms are kept, but there you have it. The reds go well with most foods, though it would be a stretch to offer them with fish and other seafoods. They go best with red foods—beef Wellington, lamb chops, steak.

The white table wines should be served chilled. (So should rosés and sparkling wines.) Served warm, they tend to taste dull. They're best offered with fish and fowl—"white" foods such as chicken breasts, fillet of sole, pheasant under glass.

Shall we get a tad more specific? Okay, here's a quick rundown of various foods you might be serving, and a few wines you might select to go along with them:

- With crackers and cheese, and most hors d'oeuvres: sherry, champagne, vermouth.
- Seafoods: white Burgundy, Chablis, dry sauterne, Moselle.
- Fowl: Rhine wine, Bordeaux, champagne, white Burgundy.
- Meats: red Burgundy, claret, a rosé (if served with cold cuts).
- Cheese or nuts (my, aren't you Continental): port, sherry, zinfandel, muscatel.
- Desserts: sweet sauterne, champagne, port, Tokay.

When you're storing wines for later use, keep the bottles in a cool, dark place, and lay them on their sides; this will keep the corks moist and tight.

If you're serving a red wine, open it an hour or two before, to give it a chance to "breathe."

If, however, you smell a cork you've just removed from a bottle, and it has a vinegary scent, the wine's gone bad. Serve something else (and save the bad wine for cooking—for which it's perfectly good).

If there's sediment in the bottle (common enough in good wines), allow the bottle to stand upright for an hour or two before serving. The sediment will settle to the bottom, and careful pouring won't disturb it.

When opening champagne, it's important to remember that the cork is not a bullet; don't allow it to ricochet around the room. (As your mother would say, "You could put somebody's eye out.") After removing the foil, and the little wire net around the neck of the bottle, drape a napkin, or cloth, over the top; this will catch the cork if it tries to fly off. Holding the cork still, gently twist the bottle. Be standing near a sink, or an ice bucket, in case there's some frothing action; to reduce frothing, and increase the sparkle, hold the bottle at a slight angle after the cork is out. In a few seconds, you're ready to pour.

When filling wineglasses, it's customary not to lift them. This means you may have to move around a bit, and pour with some accuracy. Nor should you fill the glasses more than half or two-thirds of the way to the top. Trust me, you won't look cheap—just refined.

The Dinner Party

In your heart, you know it's right.

Jack and Alice have had you to dinner twice.

Morty and June three times.

Dave and Deirdre took you on a round-the-world cruise on their private sloop.

It's time you reciprocated—with a dinner party.

First of all, don't panic. Planning and foresight will get you through just fine.

Check the calendar, and pick a date that's still a few weeks away.

Make a guest list—a nice mix of personalities and professions. Ideally, something between four and eight people.

Choose a printed invitation. Not a phone call? No. Buy printed cards, or make up your own, but do put the facts in writing and let your invitees respond.

What facts, exactly? Place and time, for sure. You might, for instance, say "Cocktails at 6:30. Dinner at 7:30." When you're serving a dinner, you do want people to know when they're expected to show up, and for what. An hour is about right for the preprandial socializing.

If there's a special occasion behind the party (a birthday, a housewarming, an anniversary), you might add that, too.

In the week or two before your dinner party, go about procuring, in a leisurely fashion, such things as the wine, the candles, the music you want playing (softly) in the background.

The day before your party, do the household clean-up.

The day before your party, pick up all the other non-perishables. If, for instance, you're serving ice cream for dessert, pick up a half-gallon and stick it in the freezer.

The day of your party (after you've awakened in a cold sweat, wondering what the hell ever possessed you to do this in the first place), get the food and start cooking. Here, three words of advice: keep it simple. Even if you're a world-class cook, when you're a host you've got loads of other responsibilities too. So fix something that's both easy to prepare and easy to serve. Lamb chops and such are lovely—but a stew, or a chili, for example, can be made before your guests even arrive. With these, it's also easy and inexpensive to make a ton of the stuff—anybody who wants seconds (or thirds) can dig in.

Consider, also, the myriad of caterers, who can bring to your house, or fix in your very own kitchen, a lovely, delicious (but often expensive) meal.

As far as the seating arrangement is concerned, you can go all the way from formal place cards (seldom necessary) to catch-as-catch-can (not always advisable either). When people go to the table, they want a little guidance as to where you want them. Customarily, the young-and-in-love couples are seated together; the old-and-already-tired-of-each-other are separated. If you're not sure which is which, ask. (Just *kidding*.)

If you like to bake, feel free to offer a homemade dessert. Otherwise, is there a town in America that doesn't have at least one decent bakery? Buy a cheesecake and serve it with fresh berries on the side; buy a selection of biscotti and serve them with Haagen Dazs and coffee. (Decaf, by the way, is what people will generally ask for these days.)

Depending on your house or apartment, you may wish to adjourn from the table to have your postprandial drinks (a brandy, a crème de menthe, an Amaretto) back in the living room. Offering a plate of after-dinner mints is a nice touch.

Do not even think about starting the clean-up or the dishes while a guest still lingers. If anyone offers to help with the dishes, decline. (They're just being polite.)

Finally, remember this: nobody comes to dinner parties for the food. (Well, almost nobody.) They come for the company—and for *your* company—and they're happy to have been asked. Even if the soufflé exploded and the napkins didn't match, your guests will remember only that they had an enjoyable evening out.

As for you, you're now off the hook for at least six months. Maybe longer.

None for the Road

Of course you want your guests to enjoy themselves at your home. But what do you do when one of them enjoys himself too much?

In short, how do you handle the inebriated guest?

Ah. If during the course of the evening he actually becomes drunk, or in any way abusive, you can try to separate him from the other guests, and the bar, for a period of time. Maybe he'll sober up. If this looks unlikely, you will have to ask him to leave.

But you can't send him out on the road like that—not if he's driving, at least. Your choices? You can ask one of the other guests to drive him home. You can call a cab, and when it arrives you can deposit your friend in the back seat, give the cabbie instructions on where to go, and then pay him yourself. Tip the cabbie generously.

Or, if you've got the room, you can put your sloshed friend up for the night. Make sure he knows where the bathroom is.

But let us suppose you've invited over a friend who you already know is a recovering alcoholic. Does that mean you have to alter everything for everyone else you've invited, from serving no wine with dinner to concealing the bar cabinet?

No. The tactful host makes only the most minimal changes. The cocktail hour, for instance, may be shortened slightly. But you should never embarrass your guest by explicitly offering him a soft drink or fruit juice. Simply ask him what he would like to drink, just as you would any other guest.

If he asks, as he no doubt will, for a glass of ginger ale or some such innocuous drink, serve it to him as you would any other drink—in the same barware you're using for everyone else, and with a festive twist of lemon or lime.

At the table, do not leave the wineglass conspicuously absent from his place. In most cases, he'll simply decline to have any wine poured into it. But he may also elect to have the glass filled (though he doesn't drink from it), just so as to call less attention to himself. It's his call.

For dessert (indeed, all through the meal), don't serve anything with a noticeable alcoholic component. To wit, skip the rum cake, the custard laced with cognac, the ice cream doused in a heavy liqueur. There are plenty of other sweets to choose from. Your friend will be grateful for your consideration, and nobody else will even notice.

The Art of Using Chopsticks

If it's any comfort, the earliest Chinese word for chopsticks was derived from the word "zi," a variation of "help." So take heart—you're not the only one who needs it.

Confronted with a pair of chopsticks, usually two splints of wood that still need to be separated, most of us react with a combination of pleasure and annoyance. We know they'll be fun and different—and we know we'll be chasing that pea pod around the plate for the next half hour.

But learning to hold and use chopsticks properly can lower your anxiety level, and optimize the fun. Here's how to do it.

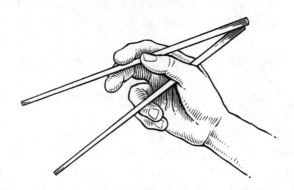

We'll call the chopsticks top and bottom. Nestle the bottom chopstick into the crook between your thumb and index finger. Use the top edge of your fourth finger to give it some support. This chopstick is there to provide solid backup for the top chopstick. The top does most of the work. It is held between the tip of your thumb and the top of your second and third fingers. It's the top chopstick that goes on the Search-and-Enjoy missions.

This is the classical method. When dining with the party chairman in Beijing, use it. When eating with friends at your local Chinese restaurant, you may find some simpler variation that works for you. Still, if you find yourself so frustrated you're ready to hurl an eggroll across the room—if you could only get hold of it—call for a fork.

Lights, Camera, Action!

Let us suppose your fifteen minutes of fame have arrived. You've been asked to appear on TV. Maybe you're booked to appear on a public affairs program, as a company spokesman; maybe you're going to show up on an afternoon talk show, discussing some intimate family secret that you've never before discussed with anyone.

Whatever the reason, if you want to make the most of your television debut, remember to:

• Show up at the studio far enough ahead of time for the makeup artist to pat you down—face, neck, hands—with foundation. And don't say no. You may think you look fine without any makeup, but if you go on the air that way, you'll look like a cadaver.

• If you're planning to wear a tie, don't make it an expensive silk one. A techie will try to attach a lavalier microphone to it, and unless he's very careful taking the mike on and off, he can shred the fabric.

• If you can help it, don't wear anything with a pattern. Lines and checks and, God forbid, plaids can bleed all over the screen. Avoid white shirts, too—they either look dingy, or they glare. Pale blue is best.

• Keep your sound bites short and pithy. TV people get alarmed when they hear any sentence with more than two clauses. Or containing words unfamiliar to a fourth-grader of average intelligence.

• After you've taken your seat on the set, take one quick glance at yourself on the monitors—Is your hair all right? Is your shirt tucked in?—and then don't look again. There's nothing quite so distracting as the sight of your own talking head.

• Never upstage the host or interviewer. Let them per-form your introduction uninterrupted, and when they head for the sign-off, stop talking. Don't try to add any little afterthought.

· TV interviews often run no more than three or four minutes. If you have a point you want to make, make it early, and make it often. You'll be out on the street again before you know it.

· Now that you're a star, don't forget the little people who helped make it happen.

"What's This Country Coming To?"

You're watching the evening news when suddenly you see it—a story that really gets under your skin. Those pointy-headed bureaucrats in Washington are about to pull another stunt that's going to cost you, the taxpayer, mucho dinero before they're done. You're mad as hell, and you're not going to take it anymore. You want to fire off a letter, quick, while you've got a head of steam up, but you don't know where to send it. You know who you voted for—at least you think you can remember—but where the heck do you find those Senators and Representatives now?

To reach your Senator, address your letter to him or her at the United States Senate, Washington, D.C. 20510.

To reach your Representative, send it to the United States House of Representatives, Washington, D.C. 20515.

If you want a more specific (or local) address for a member of Congress, go to your closest library and ask for *The Congressional Staff Directory* or *Congressional Quarterly's Washington Directory*.

But suppose it's not something of national importance that's got your goat. Suppose it's just something you saw on a TV show—an episode of *Melrose Place* that you feel went too far, a report on moral decay that didn't go far enough, a commercial you feel was in bad taste. If you're still in the mood to protest, here's where to find some of the major networks:

ABC
77 W. 66th St.
New York NY 10023
(212) 456-7477

Fox Broadcasting Company
P.O. Box 900
Beverly Hills CA 90213
(310) 277-2211

CBS, Inc.
51 West 52nd St.
New York NY 10019
(212) 975-3247

Cable Network News
P.O. Box 105264
1050 Techwood Drive
Atlanta GA 30318
(404) 827-1500

NBC
30 Rockefeller Plaza
New York NY 10112
(212) 664-4444

Words to the Wise

Your friend comes to you. He's got a problem. He needs to talk about it. He does talk. You listen. You nod. And then, after suitable reflection, drawing upon a lifetime of experience and rumination, you offer your best advice and counsel.

And he says, "Yeah. Uh-huh ... You catch the game last night? I can't believe they put Osborne back on the court."

Did you do something wrong? Has your advice been so cavalierly dismissed? If he didn't want to know what you thought, why'd he ask in the first place? Where's the gratitude?

In offering advice, you must realize that you are entering an area calling for the tact of a diplomat, the wisdom of a sage, and the patience of a saint. There are dozens of reasons people ask for advice, and dozens of reasons, not all of them pure, that people dispense it.

The first thing to keep in mind is that, most of the time, people just want to ventilate. They want to complain, they want to say all the things they couldn't say to the person they're mad at, they want to tell the world what injustices they've suffered.

And then they feel better.

Any advice you give here will fall on deaf ears. The complainants are already done; they've moved on. If you persist in talking about their problem and offering your suggestions, you will either bore them or annoy them.

And even if they *are* looking for your take on the problem, proceed with caution. Try to see the problem from their point of view—not yours. If it's a money problem and you're well off, think back to a time in your life when you were short of funds yourself. Solving their problem with your resources would be a cinch (and you can always consider a loan), but solving the problem with what they have in the bank might not be so easy.

Try, too, to acknowledge whatever values or predispositions they bring to the problem. In other words, if you're a born-again Christian, and they're a Hindu, don't tell them to run down to the river and get baptized in the name of Christ. This won't work. Nor is this the time to start proselytizing for your cause. They're looking for counsel, not conversion.

Listen carefully—and ask if they don't tell you—for what remedies they might have already tried. Why reinvent the wheel? If they've already applied for a government grant to fund their project, why try to tell them how to go about it?

Offer, if relevant, anecdotes from your own life. If you and your sister once had a similar argument, and you actually learned something from it, say so. Affirmation can be very helpful. Just don't go off on your own tangent for the next thirty minutes. You're supposed to be a supporting player in this discussion, not the star.

And before you say a word, do an internal motivation check. Are you offering the advice you're about to give with your friend's best interests at heart, or do you have some ulterior motive? If he's wondering, for instance, if he should break up with Monica, before you tell him to give her the old heave-ho, make sure that you're not planning to call her yourself as soon as he does.

That would be beneath you.

Street Fighting Man

First, let it be said that your wisest course of action—in nearly all cases of criminal violence—is to take to your heels and flee. Even the most courteous mugger may well be carrying a Beretta, and a grudge.

But suppose it's already too late for that? Suppose your opponent is threatening your corporeal well-being and at the same time making your exit impossible? Then lose not a moment. Start doing as much damage as you can, as fast as you can. A sudden offense may be your best—and only— shot at self-preservation.

The first thing to drop is your dignity. While you're wondering what's fair—closed fists? hollering? kicking?— your attacker is wondering where he's going to dump your body. So unless you consider yourself a skilled boxer, a karate master, or a wizard of jujitsu, bring up your elbows and, rotating your hips and shoulder as you do, swing them with all the power you can. Back and forth. If his head's in reach, go for it. Kick, too, if the opportunity presents itself. Go for the guy's knees—they're low enough to reach easily, they're easily damaged, and if you connect, you may still be able to make your escape when he's down.

Other areas of vulnerability? His groin, of course, but if you try kicking him there—and miss—you can wind up off balance and vulnerable; even a knee to his groin brings you into a perilously close embrace with your enemy. The eyes, of course, are a good target; a fist, or even a jabbed thumb to the eye, can vastly improve the odds in your favor. As will a karate-style chop with your forearm to his carotid artery. Or a swift hard smack, palm open, to his ear; done right, this can pop an eardrum and make it tough for him to keep his balance.

Remember: swift, decisive, and destructive blows, of any sort, are your one hope of salvation—especially because they will come as such an unexpected surprise to your attacker. Probably one of the reasons he picked on you in the first place is that he didn't count on any major resistance. (You've got to stop wearing those pocket pen-protectors and fixing your glasses with Scotch tape.) Finally, never linger to savor a victory. It could be only temporary.

The Lawful Truth

With the exception of lawyers, it should be everyone's ambition to get through life without ever getting caught up in the coils of the law. At the same time, in our increasingly litigious society, you'd probably have to live in a cave to manage it.

With that in mind, what follows is a primer in legal terminology—some of these terms may come to play a part in your own daily affairs, some you will only hear bandied about on *LA Law*. But either way, it's good to know 'em— ignorance of the law, as they say, is no excuse.

affidavit: a written statement that you submit, and swear to be true, under penalty of perjury.

deposition: if you're called upon to be a witness in a trial, you may be "deposed," or questioned, before the trial. Usually, this goes on in a lawyer's office.

arraignment: the procedure when you are called before the court, formally charged with a crime, and advised of your constitutional rights. A plea may or may not be entered at this time. (Ask Dershowitz for guidance.)

summons: a notice that you are now a party to a legal proceeding; the summons will tell you whether you are required to appear in court on a particular day, or to file a document with the court within a particular time period.

subpoena: a court writ, requiring that you show up at a specific time and place, to testify in a judicial proceeding. Be there—or be held in contempt of court.

indictment: submitted by a public prosecutor, and delivered to a grand jury, the document accusing one or more people of a crime. Try not to be one of them. If the grand jury thinks the evidence submitted is enough to warrant a trial, they will endorse the indictment—which then, like a caterpillar becoming a butterfly, is transformed into a "true bill."

amicus curiae: friend of the court; a purportedly disinterested observer, who, while not a party to the lawsuit, has an interest in its outcome.

injunction: a court order that forbids you from performing a particular act, or that may require you to perform a particular act.

corpus delicti: no, no, no, it's not what you think. It's simply the object upon which a crime has been committed. Oh, it could be the body of a blonde bombshell, but it could also be the car spray-painted with graffiti from stem to stern.

in flagrante delicto: everyone's favorite legal expression. It sounds so . . . thrilling. In fact, it just means caught in the act; red-handed.

murder: one term you hope never to hear in person—unless you're sitting in the jury box. For the record, it means homicide with malice aforethought. If you planned the murder for weeks in advance, you're likely to be charged with first-degree murder. If it was something you cooked up over a late-night bowl of microwave popcorn, and then committed without a whole lot of thought, you'll probably qualify for second-degree.

manslaughter: homicide without malice aforethought. It's called "voluntary manslaughter" if there are extenuating circumstances; for instance, if you were fighting over a parking spot that wasn't subject to alternate-side-of-the-street regulations. It's "involuntary" if you knocked somebody off through criminal negligence; for example, by accidentally driving your tractor through their living room.

circumstantial evidence: evidence that isn't based on direct observation or knowledge—nobody saw that rifle being fired—but which is implied from things we do know.

defamation: when your reputation is damaged. If you've been unjustly maligned in print, you can sue for libel; if you've been unjustly maligned in speech, you can sue for slander.

nolo contendere: when, as a defendant, you plead no contest to the charges in a case. Spiro Agnew first made the term broadly known.

Addendum: Last Rights

Uncle Bernie has . . . passed on. He was always like . . . an uncle to you. He would have been 104, this coming spring. But alas, instead of smelling the daisies, he'll be pushing them up.

Still, he has not died intestate (without leaving a will). Uncle Bernie was always careful in his affairs (with the exception of that fling with Candi, the eighteen-year-old nurse therapist he briefly married two years ago, and who agreed to leave only after a three-million-dollar payout). No, Uncle Bernie has left behind a meticulously drawn up, and witnessed, Last Will and Testament. And while nothing can ever make up to you the loss of your dear Uncle Bernie— Remember how he used to dry his hands on your hair? How he'd absentmindedly overlook your birthday every year? How he tried to French kiss your bride at the wedding?—it's time to put your grief behind you and move on with your life. When it comes to the reading of the will, some terms you may wish to know are:

estate: no, it's not just the grounds of Oakwood Manor, Uncle Bernie's gated, walled, and electrified compound in Poughkeepsie. It's everything he owned—lock, stock, and barrel.

probate: the legal process designed to establish the legitimacy of a will.

bequest: any personal property that is given as a gift is a bequest, and is bequeathed. And all property is considered personal, unless it is . . .

"real" property: real means land, or anything attached to the land, such as an apartment building. When real property is passed on, it's not bequeathed, but "devised."

codicil: a later addition to a will, altering it in some way. Watch out for these—did you send Uncle Bernie a chintzy wedding present when he married Candi? Oops. Bad planning.

executor: if you're appointed executor, it's your job to make sure that the provisions of the will are carried out. The executor is generally paid a fee, out of the estate, for this service.

Taxing Questions

With all the money you've just inherited, you've now been lifted into a new and altogether more onerous tax bracket. If you haven't got one already, it may be time to hire an accountant.

What should you look for in an accountant, and what can you expect?

First of all, what you want is a CPA (a Certified Public Accountant). That means he or she has passed rigorous state licensing tests. It also means that he won't want to do anything that could get his hard-won license revoked.

In other words, your accountant will not lie, cheat, steal, or cover for you. If you've got deep, dark secrets you don't want anyone to know, don't tell your accountant. He will prepare your taxes based on exactly what he knows about your finances.

What should he know? Ideally, everything. A good accountant can find perfectly legal, tax-saving ideas in all sorts of places. So level with him. And keep him apprised of your changing financial picture. If you've suddenly switched to a new job, with a much larger salary (God bless you), give your accountant a call. There may be things you can do right now—from deferring income to acquiring new deductions—that can lower your tax bite considerably.

What will it cost you? Accountants do not take a cut of what they save you on taxes; they assess fees on a retainer basis, or charge a straight hourly rate (the more usual method). To file federal and local returns, the fee will probably range, depending on the complexity of your taxes, from two to five hundred bucks.

Finally, remember that your tax return is yours, not his. The CPA will assume responsibility for computational or filing errors, but otherwise, it's your baby. If the IRS comes calling, with a few niggling questions about those charitable deductions you claimed, it's up to you to prove your old bowling trophies were worth $1,000 to the Little Sisters of the Poor.

Audit Etiquette

Sometimes it's something you did—a questionable deduction, missing documentation, an invisible dependent—that triggers an audit.

And sometimes it's just the luck of the draw. Bad luck. Either way, there are six rules to surviving an audit.

(1) Unless they insist, go to the IRS office—don't have the auditor come to your home. At your home, it's too easy for him to look around and see something that starts him wondering (such as the Rolls in the driveway).

(2) Bring with you only the records and documentation you'll need to settle the issue, or issues, raised in the notification of your audit. Truck in everything else, and you can inadvertently launch the auditor on a fishing expedition.

(3) Dress well. Nobody's fooled by the ratty T-shirt and jeans. But at the same time, don't *over*dress. If you wear a suit, don't make it a $2,000 Armani that your auditor himself couldn't afford. Envy is not a happy emotion to stir up in an auditor.

(4) Volunteer nothing. There's nothing wrong with being friendly—you do, after all, want to win him over a bit—but once you start burbling, there's no telling what will spill out next.

(5) Answer succinctly. A "yes" is fine, a "no" is acceptable, and even an "I'll have to check on that" is okay, but don't go yammering on. The more you rattle on, the more it looks like you have something to conceal.

(6) Don't argue with your auditor. Yes, state your case when asked, but if things actually start to get hostile, either cool down, or request a new auditor. You are perfectly within your rights to do so. Chances are, your auditor will then cool off, too—more than likely, he'd like to close this file himself, and get rid of you as quickly as possible.

It's a Dog's Life

Sure, he's your best friend—ready to romp any time you are, there to lend a consoling paw whenever you need it, always patrolling the premises—but when was the last time you asked him what his favorite foods were, what he's been dreaming about lately, or why he keeps mixing up colors? (Yes, there really are answers to these questions.)

Here, some important tips (and all of them vetted by the official publications of the American Kennel Club) to help you understand and grow closer to your pooch.

• Given their druthers, dogs would always rather have meat than a high-protein, non-meat diet. Not only that, they have meat preferences, too: in descending order, they like beef, pork, lamb, chicken, and horsemeat. (Who doesn't?)

• And they like variety. They get as bored as you would be, eating the same thing night after night.

• Dogs, according to most veterinarians, do indeed dream—and puppies most of all. If the rapid eye movements and limb twitches are any indication, hunting is a popular sleep subject.

• Dogs can see colors—but not very well. (That explains all the plaids they wear.) They have trouble distinguishing between shades of yellow and green, orange and red, but they can always distinguish these from white. They've got a much keener sense of blue, violet, and indigo.

• Dogs are sociable creatures—in fact, they even eat with greater gusto when there are other dogs around to join in the feast.

• Dogs, like humans, are right- or left-handed. Also like humans, the preponderance are righties, particularly among females. If you want to know if your own pooch is a rightie or a leftie, ask him to shake hands and see which paw he puts out.

Safety Tips

• Dogs, too, can get a sunburn. If you're heading for a day outdoors, especially the beach, apply some sunblock to his ears and nose about a half hour before going out.

• Tempting as the sea water might be, don't let your dog drink too much of it. He'll get sick from the salt, just as you would.

• Although most dogs are ardent swimmers, never just throw a dog into the water. Let him learn gradually. Try, if practicable, the buddy system—if he's got a doggie friend who already knows how, let him follow his friend's lead into the surf.

• While leaving your dog in a closed car is always to be discouraged, do remember—if you must—to leave the windows ajar, some water available, and the car parked in the shade.

• In wintertime, don't leave your dog outdoors for long stretches of time; he could get frostbite on his ears, tail, or feet.

• If you're out walking on streets sprinkled with rock salt, be aware that this could irritate your dog's footpads. When you get back home, rinse off his paws and dry them. Also, keep him away from any spots of antifreeze that may have collected in the street or on the driveway. Dogs like the way it tastes and smells, but it's highly poisonous.

• At Christmas, keep the tree and the dog apart. The needles are sharp and indigestible, the lights strung down low can get hot and burn an inquisitive pooch, and tinsel, if swallowed, can block his intestines. The holly, mistletoe, and poinsettia plants, all poisonous, should be kept out of his reach, too. For that matter, chocolate and alcohol are also toxic for dogs.

• If you're still wondering about acquiring a dog— what kind to get, how to care for him, where to go—write to the American Kennel Club at 5580 Centerview Dr., Suite 200, Raleigh, NC 27606-3390. Ask for their Responsible Dog Ownership Packet (it's free).

Bibliography

Ausubel, Nathan, ed. *A Treasury of Jewish Humor*. New York: M. Evans and Company, 1951.

Baldrige, Letitia. *Letitia Baldrige's New Complete Guide to Executive Manners*. New York: Rawson Associates, 1993.

Baldrige, Letitia. *The Amy Vanderbilt Complete Book of Etiquette*. New York: Doubleday and Company, 1978.

Beck, Emily Morison, ed. *Familiar Quotations by John Bartlett, Fourteenth Edition*. Boston: Little, Brown and Company, 1968.

Boyles, Dennis, and Alan Rose, Alan Wellikoff, eds. *The Modern Man's Guide to Life*. New York: Perennial Library, 1987.

Broder, Michael. *The Art of Staying Together*. New York: Hyperion, 1993.

Brown, George Albert. *The Airline Passenger's Guerrilla Handbook*. Washington, D.C.: The Blakes Publishing Group, 1989.

Chapman, Elizabeth, and Margaret Kassner, Karen Kriberney. *The Modern Woman's Guide to Life*. New York: Harper and Row, 1980.

Cowle, Jerry. *How to Survive Getting Fired—and Win!* Chicago: Follett Publishing Company, 1979.

Fargis, Paul, and Sheree Bykofsky, eds. *The New York Public Library Desk Reference*. New York: Stonesong Press Books, 1989.

Florman, Monte, and Marjorie Florman. *How to Clean Practically Anything*. New York: Consumer Reports Books, 1992.

Godin, Seth. *The 1994 Information Please Business Almanac and Desk Reference*. Boston and New York: Houghton Mifflin Company, 1994.

Gross, Kim Johnson, and Jeff Stone. *Chic Simple: Shirt and Tie*. New York: Alfred A. Knopf, 1993.

Johnson, Hugh. *Hugh Johnson's Pocket Encyclopedia of Wine, 1993*. New York: Simon and Schuster, 1993.

Korda, Michael. *Power!* New York: Random House, 1975.

Mackay, Harvey. *Beware the Naked Man Who Offers You His Shirt.* New York: William Morrow and Company, 1990.

Malmuth, Mason, and Lynne Loomis. *Fundamentals of Poker.* Las Vegas: Two Plus Two Publishing, 1992.

Masello, Robert. *Proverbial Wisdom.* Chicago: Contemporary Books, 1993.

McCarthy, Laura Flynn. *Every Woman's Beauty Basics.* New York: Guild America Books, 1994.

Molloy, John T. *Live for Success.* New York: William Morrow and Company, 1981.

Molloy, John T. *Dress for Success.* New York: Peter H. Wyden, 1975.

Mr. Boston Deluxe Official Bartender's Guide. New York: Warner Books, 1981.

Newmark, Maxim. *Dictionary of Foreign Words and Phrases.* New York: Philosophical Library, 1950.

Rapoport, Alan M. (M.D.), and Fred D. Sheftell, M.D. *Headache Relief.* New York: Simon and Schuster, 1990.

Scher, Bob. *The Little Know-How Book.* New York: Harmony Books, 1993.

Stewart, Marjabelle Young. *The New Etiquette.* New York: St. Martin's Press, 1987.

Sutherland, Douglas. *The English Gentleman.* London: Debrett's Peerage Ltd., 1978.

Visser, Margaret. *The Rituals of Dinner.* New York: Penguin Books, New York, 1991.

About the Author

Robert Masello is an award-winning journalist and author whose work has appeared in many prominent national publications, including *The Washington Post, New York Newsday, The Los Angeles Times, People, Redbook, TV Guide,* and *New York* magazine. He began his publishing career working for *Esquire* and *Gentlemen's Quarterly,* and later contributed the "His" column to *Mademoiselle* for five years.

His books, which have been published here and abroad (and translated into four languages), include both nonfiction and novels.

Currently, he resides with his wife in Los Angeles.